T0380720

The **Letter Kills,**
but the
Spirit Gives Life

Sky Takemoto

WESTBOW
PRESS®
A DIVISION OF THOMAS NELSON
& ZONDERVAN

WestBow Press books may be ordered through booksellers or by contacting:

WestBow Press
A Division of Thomas Nelson & Zondervan
1663 Liberty Drive
Bloomington, IN 47403
www.westbowpress.com
844-714-3454

ISBN: 979-8-3850-2897-9 (sc)
ISBN: 979-8-3850-2898-6 (hc)
ISBN: 979-8-3850-2899-3 (e)

Library of Congress Control Number: 2024914139

Print information available on the last page.

WestBow Press rev. date: 03/10/2025

CONTENTS

PREFACE

Second Corinthians 3:6 says, "The letter kills, but the Spirit gives life." Romans 2:29 says, "In spirit, not in letter." The Bible without the Spirit is the letter from the tree of knowledge of good and evil. Anything we do independently of the Lord is in the principle of the tree of knowledge. Independence means death.

The principle of the tree of life is dependence on God. John 6:63 says, "It is the Spirit who gives life." Christ is the living Word, the scriptures (*logos*) are the written Word, and *rhema* is the instant and present spoken Word. The words (rhema) spoken by the Word (logos) are the Spirit who gives life. The words that He has spoken to us are spirit and are life.

I have been burdened with a need to publish my dissertation as a book because the Spirit is one of the most important central themes in the Bible. And I wrote this book with the hope that all Christians would experience the Spirit. When readers receive the shining light and touch the Spirit, their inner being will be refreshed and renewed, and they will be filled with joy and peace. By the Spirit, they will experience the Spirit's work and enjoy the riches of Christ as the pneumatized Spirit because the Spirit is the reality of Christ.

The title of this book is *The Letter Kills, but the Spirit Gives Life*. God desires that we be in spirit. The indwelling Spirit is the key to God's economy. In the first chapter, I write about Christ as the Spirit indwelling the human spirit. The second chapter presents four primary issues concerning the Holy Spirit, and the third chapter concerns the application of the Holy Spirit to believers.

The main concept of *The Letter Kills, but the Spirit Gives Life* is that the Spirit reaches us in two ways: inwardly and outwardly. On the day of Christ's resurrection, the inward aspect was accomplished (John 20:22). On that day, the Lord Jesus, as the pneumatic Christ, came back to His disciples and breathed Himself into them as the life-giving Spirit. On the day of Pentecost, the outward aspect was accomplished when the disciples were filled with the outpouring of the Spirit (Acts 2:1–2), which was poured upon them as power like that of a strong wind. The Spirit is primarily inward light and life and outward power and work.

In terms of the completion of *The Letter Kills, but the Spirit Gives Life*, I am indebted to many dear sisters and brothers in the Lord. From my heart, I thank Carla Waxham for helping me to convey in English the deep meaning that I was seeking to express and for carefully proofreading the manuscript. I also thank Carla's husband, Harmond Waxham, for his prayers and encouragement as I pursued this work. I would like to express my sincere gratitude to Brian Chiu, who provided me with materials on Watchman Nee and gave me the most insightful comments. Thanks to Bill Buntain, who recommended valuable sources with references and explanations, and to Paul Kim, who introduced me to Brian Chiu.

I thank Dr. Shinho Kim, who gave me the first source for the writing of my dissertation, which became my source of inspiration for *The Letter Kills, but the Spirit Gives Life*. I also thank Steve Clark and our Monday prayer group members. Both Melissa Cy and Maureen Burt prayed for me, strengthened me, and encouraged me in many ways. I especially thank Dr. Peter Im for his unwavering faith in me and for energizing me to finish this work.

I am grateful for my husband, Osamu Takemoto, for encouraging me and supporting me so that I could work diligently. I am also thankful for my daughter Melody and her husband, Cory Maxwell, for making me very happy and full of joy. I give thanks and praise to our Lord Jesus Christ, who is the reality of every positive thing in the universe.

INTRODUCTION

The author's burden is that the work of the Holy Spirit be made known to Christians, especially to young people, to seeking ones who are inwardly hungry and thirsty, and to those who long for the Lord's Word in order to grow in life. When these people touch the Spirit, receive the shining light, experience the life-giving Spirit, and continually grow into the divine life unto the full knowledge of Christ, then my burden will be released.

This generation's heart is severely damaged, more than that of any generation before, by their family life, the educational system, drugs, sin, depression, oppression, and Satan's lies, among other things. According to our experience, in order to be free from the defilement of sin and the entanglement of all these negative things, we need to be strengthened by the Holy Spirit. The indwelling Spirit is working to strengthen us into our inner being. The Spirit is moving, working, and living in us to impart life into us.

In the New Testament, *pneuma* refers to the Spirit as a person. After Christ's death and resurrection, He became the *pneumatic Christ* or the *pneumatized Christ* (John 20:19). By inhaling His breath, the disciples received Him as the Spirit. According to John 20:22, Jesus breathed into His disciples and said to them, "Receive the Holy Spirit." This indicates that the Lord Jesus came to His disciples as the Spirit, as the breath, as the divine air. The Greek word *pneuma* means spirit, and pneumatology is the study of the spirit.

The Spirit with a capital *S* refers to the Holy Spirit, and the spirit with a lowercase *s* refers to the human spirit. There are two spirits within believers. Romans 8:16 says, "The Spirit Himself witnesses with our spirit that we are children of God." It is not only the Spirit of God that witnesses, but also the believer's spirit that witnesses. Romans 9:1 says, "My conscience bearing witness with me in the Holy Spirit." This proves that the human conscience is in the human spirit.

We have a regenerated human spirit. We should remember that "the letter kills, but the Spirit gives life" (2 Cor. 3:6). Apart from the Spirit, nothing can quicken fallen humans. When we believed into the Lord, our spirit was enlivened with Christ. Today if we desire to worship God, we should know and exercise our regenerated spirit. In order to worship God in the Old Testament, the Israelites had to go to Jerusalem.

In order to worship God today, where should we go? Should we go to a church building to worship? If we want to meet God and worship God, we should turn to our spirit, the designated place of worship. As long as we are in our spirit and exercising our spirit, we are giving proper worship to God wherever we are. The focus of *The Letter Kills, but the Spirit gives Life* is the Spirit with the human spirit, and therein are three chapters concerning the divine Spirit and the human spirit.

Chapter 1 discusses Christ as the Spirit indwelling the human spirit. John 4:24 says that God is Spirit. The essence of God is Spirit, the divine breath. The divine breath, which came out from God, became the spirit of life in a human being. But after Adam's fall, the Spirit of God merely worked upon people of the Old Testament as power and life, never indwelling the human spirit. But in the New Testament, the Spirit as the living person of Christ indwells the human spirit as the person's life and light and as their power and work.

Watchman Nee also distinguishes the work of the Spirit in the Old Testament from the work of the Spirit in the New Testament. "The difference between the Old Testament and the New Testament is the Holy Spirit dwelling within man [in the New Testament]."[1]

Chapter 2 addresses four primary issues concerning the Holy Spirit. The Holy Spirit is not doctrine. *The letter kills but the Spirit gives life.* The Holy Spirit is constantly flowing into us as the river of living water. This flowing of the Spirit becomes our life and our life supply so that we might gain God and grow in Him. One of the four issues is what some theologians have emphasized, specifically that the Holy Spirit descended only once, but the Spirit's descending only once is not mentioned anywhere in the Bible.

If a person says he does not need any more water because he drank a lot of water that morning, that makes no sense. A similar principle applies to the Spirit. The Spirit is not the Dead Sea but is living water (John 4:10). John 4:14 says, "But whoever drinks of the water that I will give him shall by no means thirst forever; but the water that I will give him will become in him a fountain of water springing up into eternal life."

Chapter 3 discusses the application of the Holy Spirit to believers. When believers are trained by the Lord to deny the natural life and live according to the spirit, Christ can make His home in their hearts. They are purified and sanctified by the Word of God both inwardly and outwardly, becoming not those who live by their own will, but those who are willing to cooperate with the will of God. On this point, Jeanne Guyon

---

[1] Watchman Nee, *The Collected Works of Watchman Nee (CWWN)*, vol. 41 (Anaheim: Living Stream Ministry, 1993), 157.

declared, "This is union. Divine union. The self is ended. The human will is totally passive and responds to every movement of God's will."[2]

In conclusion, God wants to work within us and supply every part of our being with all the riches of His life. God is Spirit, and whatever we do to testify of the Lord is the result of the Holy Spirit's work through our faith. "The Holy Spirit is God Himself as a living Person."[3] "Apart from the Holy Spirit, everything is dead."[4]

All human activities and efforts without the Spirit have no value before God because their source is the fallen human nature. Watchman Nee said, "To Him, all these are dead works and should remain in the grave."[5] If we are in the soul or in the letter of the law instead of in our spirit, our soul quenches the Spirit, but if we are one with the Spirit, our entire being will be filed with the light of life.

[2] Jeanne Guyon, *Experiencing the Depths of Jesus Christ* (Jacksonville, FL: SeedSowers, 1975), 133.
[3] Watchman Nee, *The Collected Works of Watchman Nee (CWWN)*, vol. 36, 178.
[4] Watchman Nee, *CWWN*, vol. 8, 97.
[5] Ibid.

CHAPTER 1
Christ as the Spirit Indwelling the Human Spirit

GENERALLY, BELIEVERS HAVE HEARD THE NAME OF THE HOLY Spirit, but they may not have heard that Christ became the life-giving Spirit through His death and resurrection, that He is working today in His heavenly ministry, and that the church carries out His heavenly administration. We will now see some of the important ministries of Christ as the Spirit.

John 7:39 says, "The Spirit was not yet, because Jesus had not yet been glorified." He had not yet finished the process of death and resurrection that He had to pass through to become the life-giving Spirit (1 Cor. 15:45). In the New Testament, this life-giving Spirit is simply called *the Spirit* (Rom. 8:16, 23). Second Corinthians 3:17 says, "The Lord is the Spirit." When believers call on the name of the Lord Jesus and receive Him, they receive the Spirit as the resurrected Christ into their own spirit. God is in Christ as the Spirit to be life to us.

First, the Spirit entering into the human spirit is greater than the creation of the heavens and the earth. This is the new creation in Christ. How wonderful it is that the divine life and nature are united and mingled with His believers! Through the mingling of the two spirits, their eyes are opened to see Christ as the incomparable One in the universe and to experience Christ as the Spirit dwelling in their spirit.

When the Lord Jesus opened the eyes of the blind man in John 9, He put clay with saliva on his eyes and sent him to the pool of Siloam to wash. After the blind man washed, he could see clearly. The Lord Jesus spat saliva on the clay, which means humans are made of clay, and what comes out of the Lord's mouth is His divine element.

The divine element mingled with human clay to heal his eyes. This is the union of God and His believers, who have received Christ's life. This union opens the eyes of the blind. The union of God and His believers is altogether a matter of the new creation, which opens us to see the spiritual reality.

We, who are of the New Testament economy, live in the new creation. Second Corinthians 5:17 says, "Whoever is a believer in Christ is a new creation." We should be thoroughly delivered from the old creation by putting off the old person and putting on the new person. In the new person, there cannot be Greek and Jew. In the new person there is only Christ (Col. 3:9-11). "In Christ, we are all God's children, and there is no distinction between male and female. This distinction does not exist at all."[6]

"When we come to the Lord and touch Him, we transcend all male and female distinctions. We are beyond gender. Before the Lord and in Christ, there is no distinction between male and female."[7] Christ has abolished the law of the commandments, ordinances, ranks in society, cultures, genders, races, and all the divisive differences of rules and religious regulations (Gal. 3:28).

[6] Watchman Nee, *The Collected Works of Watchman Nee (CWWN)*, vol. 48 (Anaheim: Living Stream Ministry, 1993), 122.
[7] Ibid.

Through the cross, by the Spirit, we are one with God in the mingling of the divine Spirit with the human spirit. This is the new creation. God's intention is to make us a new creation in Christ. Those who live in the spirit, through the spirit, and according to the spirit are the ones who live in the new creation.

Second, the Spirit is a person dwelling in our spirit, who is another Comforter. The Spirit is the pneumatic Christ. Before the Lord Jesus's death and resurrection, He promised to send the Paraclete as another Comforter. In John 14:16, Jesus said, "And I will ask the Father, and He will give you another Comforter, that He may be with you forever." This other Comforter is the Spirit who dwells in the believers' spirits.

Concerning the Paraclete, Watchman Nee often repeated that "the Spirit is the Paraclete as another Comforter."[8] The Spirit guides believers into all the reality (John 16:13); that is, the Spirit makes all that Jesus Christ is and has real to them, to those who believe in Him. Now the Lord Jesus has not only what the Father has but also all the riches in His incarnation, human living, crucifixion, resurrection, and ascension. All these riches included in the Son are received by the Spirit. The Spirit is transmitting all these riches into His chosen and redeemed people. The purpose of the Spirit's indwelling is to dispense life, which is actually God Himself, into the three parts of our entire being.

Third, "the two aspects of the work of the Holy Spirit are His inward work for life and His outward work for power for His move."[9] The inward aspect of the Holy Spirit is mainly for the growth in life. Hence, the Holy Spirit constantly imparts life into His believers to produce a metabolic change within them.

The outpouring of the Holy Spirit takes place in Acts

---

[8] Watchman Nee, *CWWN*, vol. 48, 135.
[9] Watchman Nee, *CWWN*, vol. 25, 190.

2:17–18: "And it shall be in the last days, says God, that I will pour out of My Spirit upon all flesh, and your sons and your daughters shall prophesy, and your young men shall see visions, and your old men shall dream things in dreams; and indeed, upon My slaves, both men and women, I will pour out of My Spirit in those days, and they shall prophesy." These verses speak of the outpouring of the Holy Spirit. However, we see two aspects of the Holy Spirit's ministry: the essential aspect and the economical aspect.

Fourth, the anointing is not once and for all. "Believers need a fresh anointing every day."[10] First John 2:27 says, "And as for you, the anointing which you have received from Him abides in you, and you have no need that anyone teach you; but as His anointing teaches you concerning all things."

The anointing is the Spirit moving in believers to anoint God Himself into them. The anointing is like fresh dew falling each day from our heavenly Father. The fresh dew each day becomes the divine flow of life of the Holy Spirit to supply the believers and enable them to overcome sin and to live an overcoming life on this earth.

A. The Holy Spirit Entering into the Human Spirit as Life

The first step was the Incarnation. The Word becoming flesh (John 1:14) was greater than the creation of the universe. Since Christ's death and resurrection, the Spirit has been entering into the human spirit as life. God accomplished His purpose through a two-step process. The first step was to dispense

---

[10] Watchman Nee, *The Spiritual Man (2)* (Anaheim: Living Stream Ministry, 1992), 293.

Himself into His believers, and the second step was to bring them to Him.

For four thousand years, God was God and people were people. The two were not united or mingled together. However, through these two steps, God and humankind became united and mingled together. The principle of incarnation is that God entered into His believers. The Creator entered into the creature, but the creature still could not enter into God.

The Lord Jesus lived on this earth for thirty-three and a half years. During this period, He was among people, but He had not yet dwelt in His people. Through His death and resurrection, His believers gained the ability to enter into God, and then God could enter into His believers. Now the Lord as the Spirit is in the heavens and is also in His believers.

Through Christ's death in the flesh, He accomplished redemption for humankind. Through resurrection He was transfigured to become the Spirit that He might enter into the believers (John 20:22).

Incarnation is God entering into His creation. That the Word became flesh means that God joined Himself to His creation by His incarnation. In incarnation, the flesh that God put on became His tabernacle (John 1:14). Through incarnation, Jesus became human, but as a man, He still needed to be transfigured to become the Spirit. Through Christ's death and resurrection, He became the life-giving Spirit. Now whenever people open to the pneumatic Christ, He can enter into them.

The Lord's death and resurrection can be compared to this: The seed of a flower is sown into the ground, and it will grow to have stems, leaves, and blooms. This process transforms a seed from a plain form to a beautiful form. The Lord's going was His death, and His coming was His resurrection. Through

death and resurrection, He was transfigured from the flesh to
the Spirit.

The Lord Jesus is God yet human, and also human yet God.
He is God mingled with humanity and humanity mingled with
divinity. This process enables God to give His life to us and for
us to have life because of Him. When we receive the divine life
from God, we have also received God Himself as our life. John
11:25 says, "I am the resurrection and the life," and Colossians
3:4 says that Christ is our life.

1. The Three Parts of Human Beings

The essence of God is Spirit. G. H. Pember wrote, "This breath
of life became the spirit of man, the principle of life within
him—for, as the Lord tells us, 'It is the spirit that quickeneth'—
and by the manner of its introduction we are taught that it was a
direct emanation from the Creator."[11] "The act of God breathing
life into human beings at creation is an important forerunner
of John 20:22, where Jesus breathes on the disciples and says,
'Receive the Holy Spirit.'"[12]

John 4:24 says that God is Spirit. The essence of God is
Spirit. The essence of God is also the divine breath. He is *ruach*
in the Old Testament and pneuma in the New Testament. The
Hebrew word *ruach* (רוּחַ) and the Greek word *pneuma* (πνεῦμα)
have exactly the same meaning: "breath," "wind," or "spirit."
Genesis 2:7 presents one of the earliest biblical conceptions
of the Spirit: God breathed into the nostrils of Adam, and he
became a living soul. This breath of life is the Spirit of reality.

---

[11] G. H. Pember, *Earth's Earliest Ages and Their Connection with Modern
Spiritualism and Theosophy* (Las Vegas: Alacrity, 2015), 59.
[12] Veli-Matti Kärkkäinen, *Pneumatology: The Holy Spirit in Ecumenical,
International, and Contextual Perspective* (Grand Rapids, MI: Baker
Academic, 2002), 14.

Although Genesis 2:7 uses the Hebrew word *neshamah*, the more familiar Hebrew word *ruach* is also used in this sense of life-breath (Gen. 6:17; Ezek. 37). "God created man in His own image; in the image of God, He created him; male and female He created them" (Gen. 1:27). This man is not a singular person but a corporate person, Adam.

The man was enlivened and became a living soul with a spirit. The human spirit was created by God and lives with the breath of life from God. When we call on the name of the Lord and breathe Him as the breath of life, we are refreshed, watered, and strengthened.

God made human beings of three parts, not two parts: spirit, soul, and body (1 Thes 5:23). Our Body can be seen. "Our soul is of three parts—mind, will, and emotion; and our spirit too is of three parts—conscience, fellowship, and intuition."[13] The Holy Spirit cannot dwell in any part of a human being's soul or body and not even in a person's good heart. The Holy Spirit dwells in the believer's regenerated spirit which is the deepest part of a human being.

If believers want to touch the Spirit, then they should turn to their spirits because the Spirit dwells in the regenerated believers' spirits. Human beings were made by God with three parts: spirit, soul, and body. The human spirit can contact God, receive God, and commune with God as its spiritual life and life supply. And this divine life spreads into the soul as the human's personality, thus, to express God.

Gary W. Evans clarified the tripartite being:

> The issue of dichotomy versus a tripartite view of man carries an importance that surpasses the

---

[13] Witness Lee, *Holy Bible Recovery Version* (Anaheim: Living Stream Ministry, 2003), Hebrews 4:12, footnote 3.

question of scriptural accuracy. Ephesians 3:11 tells us that in eternity past God has a purpose, and then to carry out this purpose, in time He made a plan (called God's economy, *oikonomia*, in Ephesians 1:10). According to His plan, the Trinity determined, "Let Us make man in Our image," and what He created was a three-part man with a spirit, soul, and body (Gen. 1:26; 2:7). God fashioned man to match His plan.[14]

The Bible speaks of the human spirit, but many people are still not clear about this. Some believe that humans are divided into two parts, the soul and the body. An example of this view is R. C. H. Lenski's interpretation of the distinction between soul and spirit in his discussion of 1 Thessalonians 5:23: "Man's material part can be separated from his immaterial part, but the immaterial part cannot be divided; it is not a duality of spirit and soul."[15] Lenski explained that the soul and spirit are not separate from each other.

Mary E. McDonough asserted that humankind is trichotomous:

> The terms "inner man" and "outer man," or their equivalents, are employed in modern psychology, but the psychology of the Bible is more analytical inasmuch as it indicates a subdivision of the invisible part of man, thus teaching us that man is not dichotomous but is a trichotomous being. We

---

[14] Gary W. Evans, "Experiencing the Pneumatic Christ," *Affirmation & Critique* 3, no. 1 (January 1998): 59.

[15] R. C. H. Lenski, *The Interpretation of St. Paul's Epistles to the Colossians, to the Thessalonians, to Timothy, to Titus, and to Philemon* (Minneapolis: Augsburg, 1964), 366.

find this plainly taught in 1 Thessalonians 5:23 and indicated in Hebrews 4:12 and Luke 1:46–47.[16]

First Thessalonians 5:23 reads, "The God of peace Himself sanctify you wholly, and may your spirit and soul and body be preserved complete, without blame, at the coming of our Lord Jesus Christ." Hebrews 4:12 tells us, "The word of God is living and operative and sharper than any two-edged sword, and piercing even to the dividing of soul and spirit and of joints and marrow, and able to discern the thoughts and intentions of the heart." And Luke 1:46–47 says, "Mary said, My soul magnifies the Lord, and my spirit has exulted in God my Savior."

A believer has both the human spirit and the divine Spirit, and the two work together. Romans 8:16 says, "The Spirit Himself witnesses with our spirit that we are children of God." Not only do the two spirits work together, but also they are joined together as one spirit. This is clearly stated in 1 Corinthians 6:17: "He who is joined to the Lord is one spirit." According to this verse, the two spirits become one spirit. To walk according to the Holy Spirit is to walk according to the mingled spirit, which is indwelt by the Holy Spirit.

After God created all things in the universe, God created man on the sixth day. After God created man, He placed Adam in front of the tree of life. Even before Adam, there was already God as the tree of life and Satan as the tree of knowledge of good and evil in the Garden of Eden. Before Adam was able to eat of the tree of life, Satan tempted him to eat of the tree of knowledge, and afterward, Adam received the life of Satan to fulfill Satan's evil intention.

Now, after Adam's fall, the human spirit is dead because of

---

[16] Mary E. McDonough, *God's Plan of Redemption* (Anaheim: Living Stream Ministry, 1999), 16.

sin. The fall resulted in the deadening of the human spirit. In Genesis 3, the serpent in the Garden of Eden is the embodiment of the devil; "the subtle one" signifies Satan. He was a murderer from the beginning and is also a liar (John 8:44). He is called "the tempter" (Matt. 4:3), who in a subtle and crafty way seduced the God-created humans and thereby caused them to sin and fall.

By doing this, Satan injected himself into the first Adam and caused all humankind to have the serpentine poison, and then they belonged to him (Matt. 3:7; 23:33). Ephesians 2:1–2 says, "And you, though dead in your offenses and sins, in which you once walked according to the age of this world, according to the ruler of the authority of the air, of the spirit which is now operating in the sons of disobedience." This means that the human spirit was deadened, unable to function.

Watchman Nee explained the loss of the function of the human spirit:

> Adam existed by the breath of life, which is the spirit. The spirit has God-consciousness; it knows God's voice, fellowships with God, and has a very keen knowledge of God. After Adam fell, his spirit became dead. At the beginning, God said to Adam, "In the day that thou eatest thereof thou shalt surely die" (Gen. 2:17). After Adam and Eve ate the fruit, they continued to live a few hundred years. This shows that the death that God spoke of was not only physical death. The death of Adam began from his spirit.[17]

The function of the human spirit is to contact God, receive God, and commune with God. The function of the human eyes

---

[17] Watchman Nee, *The Spiritual Man (1)* (Anaheim: Living Stream Ministry, 1992), 36.

is to see, the nose is to smell, and the ears is to hear. If people who are blind or deaf have lost the function of their eyes or ears, then those functions have become deadened. Likewise, after Adam ate of the tree of the knowledge of good and evil, his spirit was deadened. Although his body was still alive, his spirit was deadened within because he had lost the ability to contact God.

When people first sinned, this sin extinguished the keen, intuitive knowledge of God in their spirit. The deadness of their human spirit pervaded their entire being and caused them to lose the function that once enabled them to contact God. Thus, through the fall, the human soul became one with the person of Satan, the human body became Satan's dwelling place, and the human spirit was deadened. The fall of humankind ruined human beings from fulfilling God's purpose, which is to express God in His image and represent God with His dominion (Gen. 1:26).

The human body, by being corrupted in the fall, became flesh, full of lust. The real significance of the fall of Adam is that people then received Satan's thoughts, feelings, will, being, and personality in their soul. This is the real significance of the fall of humanity. Through Adam's fall, humans drifted away from God (Gen. 3:1-6), and with Cain, humans fell a further step (4:3-8). Originally, people were created to live in the spirit before God, but we fell out of our spirit and into the soul, and then we fell again from the soul to the flesh.

2. Turning Us from Darkness to Light

When God came to save sinners, He did not just take care of our transgression and of our being under His condemnation. On the contrary, when Christ was lifted up on the cross in the form of the flesh of sin, the ancient serpent Satan was judged and utterly destroyed by way of the Lord's death.

For the accomplishment of God's plan of redemption, Christ tasted death for fallen sinners, completely crucified Satan and sin, and rose again. He now works to take away the poison and to rescue people from sin and death. Only the pneumatic Christ as the Spirit, who enters into the human spirit, can cause the deadened spirit to have life and be made alive.

Once the Holy Spirit enters into the human spirit, He makes it alive. Ephesians 2 says that we were dead in trespasses and sins (v. 1), but God, who is rich in mercy, made us alive with Christ even when we were dead (vv. 4–6). When God raised the crucified Jesus from the dead, He also raised us with Him. He makes us alive by dispensing His eternal life as Christ Himself into our deadened spirit.

When God enlivens us, it is Christ Himself, who became the life-giving Spirit, who enlivens our deadened spirit. Therefore, we who receive Christ can receive the divine Spirit into our spirit. In the Old Testament, because of sin, God could not enter into the human spirit, but through the death and resurrection of Christ, we were freed from the sin of the first Adam, and we received the divine Spirit of Jesus Christ.

When we are regenerated, the first part that comes to life is the human spirit. When the Holy Spirit puts God's uncreated life into the human spirit, the human spirit is made alive (Eph. 2:5). This is like turning on a lamp. The work of the Holy Spirit begins within us and works from the center out to the circumference, from the spirit to the soul and then to the body. When our spirit is revived, we become sensitive to sin and begin to seek God.

Even though we have fallen because of our sins, we can be saved. Our salvation is related to regeneration. If we are regenerated, then we have been saved. John 1:13 says, "Who were begotten not of blood, nor of the will of the flesh, nor of the will of man, but of God." Regeneration means that God has entered into our spirit and has become our life.

Every saved person has two births. The first birth is of one's parents and is of the flesh, whereas the second birth is of God and is of the divine life. A saved person is born again of God and is a separated and sanctified person in the eyes of God. We know that a saved person has been awakened by the Holy Spirit and begins to seek after the Lord Jesus.

The Lord Jesus, the Son of God, has come and has given us understanding so that we might know the real and genuine God. In the fallen human condition, the human spirit was deadened and the human mind was darkened. Hence, our natural being without regeneration does not have the ability to know God. In fact, it is impossible for us, with a deadened spirit and a darkened mind, to know the invisible God.

Acts 26:18 says, "To open their eyes, to turn them from darkness to light and from the authority of Satan to God, that they may receive forgiveness of sins and an inheritance among those who have been sanctified by faith in Me." God opened the eyes of His believers to believe in the works of the Lord Jesus and to receive Him. Christ has come in the flesh; He accomplished redemption for sinners, and when anyone repents and believes in Him, that person receives Him.

Now that the believers' sins have been forgiven, their darkened mind has been enlightened, and their deadened spirit has been enlivened. Not only that, but also the Spirit of reality, the Spirit of revelation, has come into their being. This means that the spirit of reality has been added to their regenerated spirit to enlighten their mind.

Now they have a living spirit with the Spirit of reality

revealing spiritual realities to them. As a result, they surely have an understanding and are able to know the one true God. Before being saved, they did not have this understanding, but the Son of God has come to them and has given them this understanding so that they may know God. This understanding includes the enlightenment of their mind, the enlivening of their spirit, and the revealing of the Spirit of reality.

In John 3:3, the Lord Jesus said, "Unless one is born anew, he cannot see the kingdom of God." We need to be born anew in order to enter into the kingdom of God, which is the reign of God, a divine realm to be entered into that requires divine life. Only the divine life can realize divine things. Hence, if we desire to enter into the kingdom of God, we must be regenerated with divine life.

John 3:5 says, "Unless one is born of water and the Spirit, he cannot enter into the kingdom of God." To be regenerated is to be born of the Holy Spirit. When God as the Spirit enters into us, we receive God as life and are born anew. John 3:6 says, "That which is born of the flesh is flesh, and that which is born of the Spirit is spirit."

When the Holy Spirit enters into us, He enters into our spirit and causes us to be born anew. The first reference to Spirit in the foregoing verse is to the Holy Spirit, and the second reference to spirit is to the human spirit. Regeneration does not produce a person of flesh and blood but a person with an enlivened spirit. This verse proves that God regenerates us in our spirit. God is Spirit, and He enters into our spirit, causing us to be born again.

Andrew Murray testified of the born-again spirit:

> Jesus said, "That which is born of the Spirit is Spirit" (John 3:6). This indicates that the divine Spirit begets the new spirit in man. The two are distinguished in

> Romans 8:16: "(God's Spirit) beareth witness with
> our spirit that we are the children of God." Our
> spirit is the renewed, born-again spirit. Dwelling in
> us is God's Holy Spirit, yet He is to be distinguished
> from our spirit, witnessing in and through it.[18]

Second Timothy 3:16 says that all scripture is God-breathed. So, the Word of God is the breath of God: God's speaking is God's breathing. By breathing in the Lord Jesus, the human race can drink Him in and breathe Him. Spiritually speaking, believers' breathing is their drinking, and their drinking is their eating. When believers breathe the Lord as the divine pneuma, they drink the living water and eat Jesus as the heavenly food.

Although our human spirit has been made alive by God's salvation, we still live in the flesh. Our spirit is not yet mature or strong enough. Furthermore, because of an ignorance of spiritual matters, we may not even know that we should serve God in the spirit and not in the flesh. Therefore, after we are saved, we serve God according to our own preferences and choices, serving Him only somewhat in spirit.

The flesh includes a human being's fallen body and soul. After the spirit became deadened by the fall, the soul became the decision-maker, causing people to be independent from God. The human body became the flesh because of its lusts and the sin deriving from Satan. Since the human soul is subject to the lusts of the body, it has become fleshly. Therefore, in the scriptures, flesh denotes all the soulish and fleshly things outside the spirit. Since all things outside the spirit are the flesh, to serve God by anything outside the spirit is to serve God by the flesh.

John 6:63 says, "It is the Spirit who gives life; the flesh profits

---

[18] Andrew Murray, *The Spirit of Christ* (New Kensington, PA: Whitaker House, 1984), 7.

nothing; the words which I have spoken to you are spirit and are life." He who is the Spirit is Christ Himself in resurrection, and this Spirit is the life-giving Spirit. This indicates that the Holy Spirit, who is Christ Himself in resurrection (1 Cor. 15:45; 2 Cor. 3:17), is the holy breath—the pneuma (2 Cor. 20:22). Christ came in the flesh as the incarnate Word, and in resurrection, He became the holy pneuma, the holy breath, to breathe Himself into His disciples.

3. The Spirit of God Purposefully upon Believers in OT

For charismatic ability, ruach can come powerfully upon a human being (Judg. 14:6; 1 Sam. 16:13) and equip that person for powerful work. In the Old Testament, the ruach came upon to give life and do powerful works. But the ruach did not dwell in a human being forever.

Watchman Nee first contrasted the work of the Spirit in the Old Testament with the Spirit's work in the New Testament among believers. He asserted that there is no case in the Old Testament of the Spirit dwelling in a human spirit after Adam's fall.

The Spirit was merely working upon people, but the Spirit never dwelled in them. First Samuel 19:20 says, "So Saul sent messengers to seize David; and when they saw the company of prophets prophesying and Samuel standing and presiding over them, the Spirit of God came upon Saul's messengers, and they also prophesied." Even though they prophesied, their spirit was still dead, and the Spirit of God could not dwell within them.

> The Old and New Testaments show us that the work
> of the Holy Spirit is threefold: first, He gives people
> life; second, He dwells in people as life; and third,
> He falls upon people as power. These three include

all the aspects of the work of the Holy Spirit. In Old
Testament times there were only the first and the
third of these aspects, but not the second. For at
that time the Holy Spirit did not dwell in men. The
difference between the Old and New Testaments
lies in this second aspect, that is, in the indwelling
of the Holy Spirit.[19]

Even though the work of the Spirit of God is very powerful
in the Old Testament, the Spirit never indwelled humans.
Because of sin, the human spirit died, leaving no place for the
Spirit of God to dwell within them.

The Spirit gave life through His Word and gave power for
His work to leaders or warriors. The powerful work of the Holy
Spirit is particularly visible in Judges, which tells of several
charismatic warriors such as Othniel (3:10), Gideon (6:34),
Jephthah (11:29), and Samson. God poured out His Spirit upon
these men as clothing and equipped them with power to do His
work in specific situations.

Veli-Matti Kärkkäinen discusses the Spirit in the Old
Testament as a charismatic power in his book *Pneumatology*:

> God as life-giving Spirit is the proper source of
> life and strength; in a derivative sense, *ruach* also
> denotes "life force" (Num. 16:22). That life force
> is lacking in idols (Jer. 10:14), but it is in God (Ps.
> 33:6) and in the Messiah (Isa. 11:4). God is the
> only one who gives the life force (Isa. 42:5).[20] As a
> charismatic power, *ruach* can come mightily upon

---

[19] Watchman Nee, *The Communion of the Holy Spirit* (New York: Christian
Fellowship, 1994), 49.

[20] Veli-Matti Kärkkäinen, *Pneumatology*, 17, quoted in Eric Sjöberg, s.v.
"pneuma, pneumatikos," *Theological Dictionary of the New Testament* 6:
386–87).

a human being (Judg. 14:6, 19; 1 Sam. 16:13) and
"clothe" (equip) that person for powerful works (as
with Samson).[21]

In Judges chapters 6–8, Gideon listened carefully to the
Word of God. In order to select Gideon's three hundred men,
the Lord tested them by taking the remaining ten thousand to
the water's edge to drink. Those who knelt down and lapped
like dogs were sent home (Judg. 7:5). Only three hundred men
who could lap the water with their hands and hold it in their
mouths were chosen by God for the war against Midian (v. 6).

Jehovah told Gideon that He would deliver them from
Midian through the three hundred people. And indeed, God
delivered Israel from Midian through Gideon. Like Gideon,
these three hundred men were willing to sacrifice themselves
in order to be used by God.

> Jehovah tested the remaining ten thousand by
> bringing them to the water to drink. Those who
> bowed down on their knees and lapped as a dog laps
> were sent home (v. 5). Only the three hundred who
> lapped the water into their mouths with their hands
> were chosen by God for the battle against Midian
> (v. 6). Jehovah told Gideon that through the three
> hundred men who lapped in that way, He would
> save them from Midian. Like Gideon, these three
> hundred were willing to sacrifice in order to be used
> by God.[22]

During the time of Judges, the Spirit of God came upon
Gideon to give him life and charismatic power, but after his

---

[21] Ibid., 16–17.

[22] Witness Lee, *Life-Study of Judges* (Anaheim: Living Stream Ministry,
1996), 24.

great success, he failed miserably. This was because the Spirit of God did not indwell him, and he lived out the fallen human nature and fleshly desires. In the Old Testament, the Spirit of God came upon a person and could also leave the person.

In the New Testament, the Spirit still comes upon believers, but primarily, the Spirit indwells them and never leaves them (John 14:16). The indwelling Spirit gives life by imparting Christ into their inner beings. Even in the New Testament, if believers do not turn to the spirit, they can still wander in sins. We should set our minds on the spirit (Rom. 8:6).

Andrew Murray said that there is a twofold working of God's Spirit:

> In the Old Testament, we have the Spirit of God coming upon men and working on them in special times and ways. In the New, we have the Holy Spirit entering men and women, dwelling within them, and working from within them. In the former, we have the Spirit of God as the Almighty and Holy One. In the latter, we have the Spirit of the Father of Jesus Christ.[23]

There are several verses where the Old Testament says that the Spirit came "upon" believers. First Samuel 19:20 says, "Saul sent messengers to seize David; and when they saw the company of prophets prophesying and Samuel standing and presiding over them, the Spirit of God came upon Saul's messengers, and they also prophesied." So, Saul went there, "and the Spirit of God came upon him as well, and he went on and prophesied until he came to Naioth in Ramah" (v. 23).

When Saul was attempting to capture David by force, the Spirit of God came upon Saul's messengers and eventually upon

---

[23] Andrew Murray, *The Spirit of Christ*, 5.

Saul himself, "causing them involuntarily to fall to the ground and to prophesy for hours, thus defeating Saul's purpose and humiliating him in response to his malicious show of force against David and Samuel."[24]

In the Old Testament, the Spirit of God came upon the human race directly from God. The Spirit of God continually descended upon the human race as the divine power that moved certain people to work for God, fight for God, and speak for God, but He did not indwell any human being permanently. However, the indwelling Spirit began to dwell in believers from the start of the New Testament age. Witness Lee wrote this about the indwelling Spirit: "Now the Spirit of God together with the life of God (He is the life of God itself) dwells in our spirit so that the three—He Himself, the life of God, and our spirit—may be mingled as one and never be separated."[25]

4. Christ as the Holy Pneuma Entering into the Human Spirit

In the New Testament, the Spirit is both the Spirit of power and the Spirit of life, and furthermore, the Spirit dwells in His believers. He not only descends upon human beings, causing them to obtain God's power outwardly, but also enters into a human being as the person's inner life.

When the Spirit of God comes upon a person, He touches the individual's inner being, causing the person to repent and receive the Lord Jesus. The Holy Spirit enters into the believer's spirit to dwell within it eternally. Hence, those of us who have the Holy Spirit's indwelling have God's eternal life. The eternal

---

[24] Wayne Grudem, *Systematic Theology* (Grand Rapids, MI: Zondervan, 1994), 637.
[25] Witness Lee, *The Collected Works of Witness Lee (CWWL)*, 1940-1951, vol. 3 (Anaheim: CA, Living Stream Ministry, 2018), 340.

life of God is given to us in Christ and is mingled with our spirit.

One day after I was regenerated, I heard from my classmate that I had eternal life. At that time, I was distressed to hear that I would be living forever with the fallen human nature. However, through studying the Bible, I realized that this eternal life is different from my fallen soul life. I learned that the Lord's Words are spirit and are life (John 6:63) and that when the dead spirits hear the voice of the Son of God, they will live and be enlivened.

I realized that when we receive the Lord, the Holy Spirit comes, and when we pray, we breathe in the Spirit, and the Spirit is the eternal life, and enlivens us. When I read the Bible, I was impressed by Ezekiel 37. Before God regenerated us, we were not only sinful and filthy but also dead like dry bones, buried in graves (vv. 1-4).

When Ezekiel prophesied, the Holy Spirit worked, and there was a noise and a rattling. Verse 7 says, "As I prophesied, there was a noise, and suddenly, a rattling, and the bones came together, bone to its bone." When Ezekiel prophesied to the dead bones, the breath of life came into them. Then they became alive and stood up on their feet, and it was an exceedingly great army (37:10).

I applied what I read to my spiritual experience. When God came into me, the Holy Spirit came into me like the wind, and when I called on the name of the Lord and breathed Him in, the life-giving Spirit came into me. I was fully released by the holy pneuma, the divine indestructible life. Since then, I have been using my spirit to contact the Lord, to receive the divine life, and I am becoming one of the members of the Body of Christ.

John 3 tells us that the Lord Jesus told Nicodemus that the Spirit is like the wind, which blows where it wills and cannot be seen but can be realized by its sound (v. 8). On the day of Resurrection, the Lord Jesus came back to the disciples in the evening (20:19) and breathed into them, telling them to receive the Holy Spirit (v. 22). On the day of Pentecost, there was a sound out of heaven as of a rushing violent wind (Acts 2:2), which was the blowing of the Spirit, the heavenly ruach or pneuma.

We received the life of God through the Spirit of God, who is the Spirit of life. It is the Spirit who gives the life of God to believers (2 Cor. 3:6). Romans 8:16 says, "The Spirit Himself witnesses with our spirit that we are children of God." The believers have the Spirit within them, being conformed by the Spirit and witnessing with their spirit that they are children of God. Although they may be sinful, worldly, and weak, and although they may fall and commit sins against God, they still have the feeling that they are children of God. They spontaneously call on the name of the Lord Jesus.

This is proof that they have the Spirit of the Son witnessing in their spirit, which is the innermost and deepest part of their being. Even after they sin against God, they still sense in the innermost and deepest part of their being that they are children of God. They may feel sorrowful and ashamed of what they have done, yet they still sense in their innermost depths that they are children of God.

We also have received the Lord Jesus Christ as the holy breath, the holy pneuma as the life-giving Spirit, and now He is in us. The way to enjoy the living pneuma is to call on the name of the Lord Jesus. The reality of the name of Jesus is the Spirit. As the breath, it is very easy for Him to get into us, and as the air, it is very easy for us to get into Him. Christ in resurrection became a Spirit. This life-giving Spirit is the all-inclusive One. This all-inclusive Spirit is the all-inclusive Christ Himself, and this Christ as the Spirit is the new garment for us to wear.

Galatians 3:27 reads, "As many of you as were baptized into Christ have put on Christ." Because Christ is the pneuma as the Spirit, we can easily be immersed in Him. Christ is the all-inclusive Spirit; when we are baptized into Him, we put Him on. Immediately, He as the Spirit becomes our clothing and our covering. Christ is no longer the untreated cloth; He is now the finished garment. In this finished garment we have redemption, resurrection power, and all the divine elements of the divine person. This new garment is not just a piece of clothing but the divine pneuma, the all-inclusive Spirit.

B. Christ as the 1st Comforter and the Spirit as the 2nd Comforter

Second, the Spirit of reality as another Comforter is a person. Also, the Spirit is the breath of Christ. This other Comforter is not another person, but the same person transfigured into another form. When Jesus was on the earth, He promised His disciples the Spirit of reality as another Comforter. In John 14–16, before His death and resurrection, Jesus promised to send the Paraclete as another Comforter: "And I will ask the Father, and He will give you another Comforter, that He may be with you forever."

Veli-Matti Kärkkäinen describes the term *Paraclete*:

> One of the most distinctive features of Johannine pneumatology is the introduction of the Spirit as "another advocate" (or "other Paraclete," John 14:16), obviously implying that Jesus is the first (1 John 2:1). The term *parakletos* (from *para* + *kalein*) basically refers to "one called alongside to help," thus an advocate or defense attorney. While the Paraclete

acts as a defender of the disciples, the Paraclete's role is also that of a prosecuting attorney proving the world guilty.[26]

In John 14:16, the Lord Jesus said, "I will ask the Father, and He will give you another Comforter, that He may be with you forever." The Greek word rendered "Comforter" here is *parakletos* (παράκλητος), and *Paraclete* is the anglicized form of this Greek word. In Greek, *parakletos* denotes someone alongside who takes care of another's cause and affairs. In ancient times a paraclete was a helper, advocate, counselor, or intercessor. In John, the description includes the concept of an advocate or an attorney who takes care of His believer's case. Christ is the first Comforter, and the Spirit is another Comforter.

After resurrection, the Lord, who manifested Himself to the disciples, was the real Comforter as the breath who dwelt in His disciples. Today, believers not only have an outward Christ but also have an inward Christ. They have the *parakletos* dwelling within them for their practical daily lives and daily living. Second Corinthians 3:17 says, "The Lord is the Spirit; and where the Spirit of the Lord is, there is freedom." The Lord Jesus is the Spirit.

Believers can no longer see the incarnated Christ, but they can experience the pneumatic Christ as having a different form yet being the same person. Christ could not be with them forever in the flesh. But the other kind is to be like this One. Another Comforter is to be with them forever. This other Comforter is the Holy Spirit, whom the world cannot receive because it neither sees Him nor knows Him.

---

[26] Veli-Matti Kärkkäinen, *Pneumatology*, 21.

1. Christ as the First Paraclete

The move of God within the human race is unparalleled in history. Before the Incarnation, the Spirit of God moved only with human beings and among human beings. It was not until the age of the New Testament that God entered into human beings. God entered the womb of a human virgin (the Virgin Mary) and stayed there for nine months to be born, laying the foundation for His further move on this earth.

God entered into the Virgin Mary and was born of the woman. All human beings are the seed of man and born in sin, but Christ was the seed of woman born without sin. This means that Christ alone had a sinless life, lived a holy life, died and shed His blood for us, nullified death, swallowed death in resurrection, and destroyed the devil (Col. 2:14–16; 1 John 3:8).

After His birth, He passed through a human life of thirty-three and a half years, and He was crucified on the cross as a man. Through His all-inclusive death, He solved the problems of sin, Satan, the world, the old creation, the old man, and the flesh, in addition to all the ordinances of the law and all the differences between nations, races, societies, and social ranks. He solved all the negative problems. Finally, He released the eternal life of God. He went to the cross and died there for the accomplishment of God's eternal redemption of the human race.

Following a three-day burial, Jesus rose up from the dead. In His resurrection as the last Adam, He became the life-giving Spirit for the imparting of His divine life into His believers. Before His resurrection, Christ was the only begotten Son of God (John 3:16), but in resurrection He was born the firstborn Son of God (Acts 13:33; Rom. 8:29).

Jesus was begotten by God in His resurrection to be the

firstborn Son of God among many brothers (Rom. 8:29). He was the only begotten Son of God from eternity (John 1:18; 3:16). Through death and resurrection, He was begotten by God in His humanity to be God's firstborn Son. Through Christ's resurrection, all God's chosen people were regenerated to be the many children of God.

Without resurrection, we could not be saved and would still be in our sins under death. Without resurrection, we would have no hope and would be under the control of Satan, waiting for the final coming of death. Without the resurrection, human life here would have no meaning. Death cannot hold the resurrection life. Our hope is Christ Himself.

Christ is the believers' Paraclete, Advocate, Comforter, and Intercessor. John 14:16-17 says, "I will ask the Father, and He will give you another Comforter, that He may be with you forever, even the Spirit of reality." The Spirit as another Comforter would seem to be another person because a comforter is a person.

Hebrews 9:14 says that Christ offered Himself to God through the eternal Spirit. Christ brought every negative thing with Him to the cross and ended it, but He remains the same because He is the eternal Spirit. Though all things were ended on the cross, His Spirit could never be ended. The Lord Jesus is the eternal Redeemer, the living Person and the first Comforter. When He became the life-giving Spirit, He became another Comforter, the Spirit of reality, and the real Person in our spirit.

In W. H. Griffith Thomas's book, *The Holy Spirit of God*, he quoted Denney and Clemance as follows:

> Both the masculine pronouns, αὐτός and ἐκεῖνος, and also the function ("He shall teach") represent the Holy Spirit as personal with a definiteness hitherto unnoticed. It is particularly noteworthy

that the same term *Paraclete* is used by Saint John
of Christ Himself (1 John 2:1). So that there are two
Paracletes, each possessing a relation to the life of
believers, and both together completing the idea of
eternal and permanent redemption.[27]

The other Comforter, the Spirit of reality, is the Spirit
spoken of in John 7:39: "He said concerning the Spirit, whom
those who believed into Him were about to receive; for the
Spirit was not yet, because Jesus had not yet been glorified." The
Lord's promise concerning the giving of another Comforter
was fulfilled on the day of His resurrection, when the Spirit was
breathed into the disciples as the holy breath.

The same word is used concerning the Lord Jesus in 1 John
2:1, where it is translated as "Advocate." These are not two
separate beings; they are one. As our Advocate, Jesus is with
the Father, and as our Comforter, He is within us. There is One
within believers who takes care of all their needs.

The Lord Jesus said that His going would be the Comforter's
coming, who was spoken of as the Paraclete. "He will give
you another Comforter that He may be with you forever, even
the Spirit of reality, whom the world cannot receive, because
it does not behold Him or know Him; but you know Him,
because He abides with you and shall be in you" (John 14:16–
17). This implies that not only did God stay among people as the
incarnated Jesus, but also that He wanted to dwell in believers
as a mutual abode.

---

[27] W. H. Griffith Thomas, *The Holy Spirit of God* (Grand Rapids, MI: Wm.
B. Eerdmans, 1972), 65–66, quoted in Clemance, *The Scripture Doctrine of
the Holy Spirit*, ch. 2. See also note 1, p. 279.

2. Passing Through Death and Resurrection

There was a great distance between God and His people, but through the incarnation of the Lord Jesus, many people were able to know God and commune with Him. John 14:3 says, "And if I go and prepare a place for you, I am coming again and will receive you to Myself, so that where I am you also may be."

Furthermore, John 14:18 says, "I will not leave you as orphans; I am coming to you," which proves that the Lord's going (through His death and resurrection) was His coming to His disciples (John 14:18, 28). "He came in the flesh (1:14) and was among His disciples, but He could not enter into them while He was in the flesh. Jesus had to take the further step of passing through death and resurrection in order to be transfigured from the flesh into the Spirit that He might come into the disciples and dwell in them, as revealed in vv. 17–20."[28]

The Lord's intention was to bring human beings into God so that he may have a dwelling place within them. In order to carry this out, there were things the Lord had to accomplish first. The footnote for John 14:3 says:

> But between man and God there were many obstacles, such as sin, sins, death, the world, the flesh, the self, the old man, and Satan. For the Lord to bring man into God, He had to solve all these problems. Therefore, He had to go to the cross to accomplish redemption so that He might open the way and make a standing for man, that man might enter into God. This standing in God, being enlarged, becomes the standing in the Body of Christ.[29]

[28] Witness Lee, *Holy Bible Recovery Version* (Anaheim: Living Stream Ministry, 2003), John 14:3, footnote 1.
[29] Ibid.

For accomplishing redemption, the Lord Jesus passed through crucifixion and burial. Through His death and resurrection, He brought His disciples into Himself. The way for believers to enter into God is through the Lord Himself, who is life to them. The Lord Himself is the Spirit, the Paraclete. As the Paraclete, Christ takes care of us, including all our problems and responsibilities.

In ascension, Jesus Christ is the Advocate. First John 2:1-2 says, "My little children, these things I write to you that you may not sin. And if anyone sins, we have an Advocate with the Father, Jesus Christ the Righteous; and He Himself is the propitiation for our sins, and not for ours only but also for those of the whole world." He is the Righteous One who is the believers' Advocate. The Lord's promise concerning the giving of another Comforter was fulfilled on the day of His resurrection when the Spirit was breathed into the disciples as the holy breath.

According to John 20, this second Comforter is actually the breath of the first Comforter. Verse 22 says that the Lord breathed into His disciples and told them to receive the Holy Spirit. The Lord's breath is called the Holy Spirit, who is another Comforter. When the believers have the Spirit as Christ's breath, they can experience the Spirit as another Comforter. In John 20 the Holy Spirit is the breath of Christ.

According to John 20:22, the Lord Jesus breathed into the disciples and said to them, "Receive the Holy Spirit." This is the fulfillment of the promise in John 14-16. When this other Comforter had entered into the disciples, they realized that the Son was in the Father, the Father was in the Son, the Son was in the disciples, and the disciples were in the Son as the pneumatic Christ. They also came to realize that these three are within one another and that they each coinhere one with the others.

Christ's invisible presence is just the Spirit in His resurrection, whom He breathed into the disciples and who would be with them all the time. After the Lord Jesus breathed Himself as the Spirit into the disciples, He did not leave them essentially,[30] but He disappeared from them economically.[31] He was there when He appeared, and He was there when He disappeared. There were no more limitations of time and space.

In Watchman Nee's writing, he quoted T. Austin-Sparks as follows:

> Brother Sparks had two words about the Lord and resurrection: It is not His coming but His appearing; it is not His going, but His disappearing. Since His resurrection, nothing can confine Him. In Christ Jesus nothing can limit Him, neither death, nor time, nor space, nor anything else. Not only that, after He was resurrected, the Lord Jesus was exalted by God to the highest place, seated in heaven at the Father's right hand, "far above all rule, and authority, and power, and dominion, and every name that is named, not only in this world, but also in that which is to come" (Eph. 1:20-21).[32]

Now the Lord is not limited by believers' experience and knowledge or by time and space as when Christ had a physical body on earth. When He was on the earth, He could not be in Galilee and Judea simultaneously, but when He became the pneumatic Christ, He was able to appear anytime and anyplace to see His disciples again and again.

---

[30] Essentially means the intrinsic essence for life. The essential aspect of the Spirit is breathed into believers as life for their living.
[31] Economically means the outward element for power. The economical aspect of the Spirit is poured out upon them as power for their work.
[32] Watchman Nee, *The Communion of the Holy Spirit*, 22-23.

In Luke 24, two disciples were on the way to Emmaus, and Jesus came to talk with them. In John 20, He appeared again to the disciples, and another time He appeared and spoke to Thomas. In John 21, Jesus appeared again to the disciples at the Sea of Tiberias while they were fishing.

These various demonstrations are very particular and specific experiences of the Lord as the Spirit who dwells within His believers. It is the same with the Lord and His believers today. Sometimes He appears, and sometimes He is hidden. Sometimes believers feel that the Lord is indeed with them, while at other times they do not know where He has gone.

3. The Spirit as Another Paraclete

The Holy Spirit is the Comforter. He is the believers' Patron, Attorney, and Interpreter. As the Interpreter, He makes it easier for us to "converse" with the Father and the Son. The Son was the first Paraclete, and now the Spirit is another Paraclete. Through this One, the other Paraclete, everything concerning the Father and the Son is made understandable. The coming of the Holy Spirit is the coming of the Lord Jesus Himself.

When Jesus was still in the flesh, He said, "I am in the midst of you," not "I am in you." Only after Jesus was raised from the dead and transfigured into the Holy Spirit could He enter into His believers. This transfiguration of His is the "another Comforter" sent by God. The coming of the Holy Spirit is the coming of the Father, the Son, and the Spirit.

When the Lord breathed into the disciples on the evening of the day of His resurrection, He breathed the Holy Spirit into them, and when the Holy Spirit entered into them, both the Father and the Son were also in them. The disciples realized that the Son was in the Father, that they were also in the Son, and that the Son was in them.

Sinclair B. Ferguson declared that the Spirit dwells on and in believers:

> The Spirit's coming inaugurates a communion with Christ in which the Spirit who dwelt on Christ now dwells on and in believers. This element is brought out in the farewell discourse, when Jesus promises the disciples "another Paraclete" who will be his economic equivalent because he is his own Spirit. Jesus himself will come back to them (John 14:18), not only in the resurrection but in this new way.[33]

This perspective illumines the force of what is said in John 16:7: "I tell you the truth, it is expedient for you that I go away; for if I do not go away, the Comforter will not come to you; but if I go, I will send Him to you." This Spirit, sent by the Son and coming with the Father, testifies concerning the Son. Therefore, the disciples testify of the Son and the Father by the Spirit.

Sinclair B. Ferguson emphasized that the Spirit is fully qualified to testify of the Lord Jesus:

> The disciples and the Spirit share the essential qualification for authoritative witness-bearing. In our Lord's culture, trials were conducted not by lawyers acting for the prosecution and the defense, but by a judge eliciting the truth from witnesses who came forward with evidence (cf. Deut. 17:6). In such a context the "advocate" or "defense counsel" sought by an accused person was not a highly trained

---

[33] Sinclair B. Ferguson, *The Holy Spirit* (Downers Grove, IL: InterVarsity, 1996), 71.

> professional, but someone who would vindicate him
> or her by telling the truth.[34]

Practically speaking, when the believers call on the Lord a few times, they will feel the presence of the Lord as the Spirit. The Spirit is another intercessor, a living person, and is the breath of Christ. This living person is the Lord Himself. The Spirit as another Paraclete is the person, the Comforter, and the breath of Christ.

John reveals that we have been united with, mingled with, and even incorporated into the Triune God.[35] In John 14:20, Jesus said, "In that day you will know that I am in My Father, and you in Me, and I in you." The Lord's asking the Father to give the disciples another Comforter implies that He was the first Comforter.

We have two Comforters, the Lord Jesus and the Spirit of reality, and there are two aspects, the visible presence and the invisible presence. The two Comforters are one person in different stages. The first Comforter was Jesus in the flesh in the stage of His incarnation. He comforted His disciples and walked, lived, and acted together in a very human way. He was among the disciples and with them, but He was not yet indwelling them.

Through death and resurrection, He became the second

---

[34] Ibid., 36–37.

[35] The Triune God is the Father, the Son, and the Holy Spirit. Matthew 28:19 says, "Go therefore and disciple all the nations, baptizing them into the name of the Father and of the Son and of the Holy Spirit." Second Corinthians 13:14 says, "The grace of the Lord Jesus Christ and the love of God and the fellowship of the Holy Spirit be with you all." These verses speak of the Trinity: Jesus Christ the Son, God the Father, and the Holy Spirit. The way the Triune God is mentioned indicates that we need to enjoy the Father, the Son, and the Spirit as love, grace, and fellowship instead of as logos.

Comforter as the life-giving Spirit. The first Comforter came back in another form as the second Comforter. This is the second stage of the invisible presence. As the life-giving Spirit, He could be in the disciples and they could be in Him.

John 14 through 17 reveals the divine Trinity. The Father, the Son, and the Spirit are one God. The great sign is that believers are one in the Triune God. The believers are kept in the Father's name, they are sanctified in the Word of God, and they become one in the glory of God. Thanks to John 14 through 17, we now consider three facets to describe the believers' relationship with the Triune God: "union, mingling, and incorporation."[36]

Union is when two lives are united to become one life. Believers grow in the divine life by uniting with the divine life of the Lord. As Romans 11 says, a wild olive tree is grafted into the root of fatness of the olive tree and grows with the sap of the cultivated olive tree. This description portrays the life union of Christ and His believers.

Mingling is when two natures are united to become one nature. As we are saturated with the divine nature of Christ, we are transformed into the divine nature. God's divine nature is love, light, holiness, and righteousness.

In Leviticus 2, the meal offering is made by mingling the fine flour and the oil to create a cake for an offering to God. The fine flour refers to the Lord's fine humanity, and the oil refers to the Lord's divinity. This means that the Lord's divine attributes and our human virtues are mingled together to express His divine attributes through our human virtues.

Incorporation is when two persons are incorporated with each other to become one person. Just as the Lord dwells in the Father and the Father dwells in the Lord, we believers dwell

---

[36] Witness Lee, *CWWL*, 1994-1997, vol. 3, 577.

in the Lord and the Lord dwells in us, His believers, thereby expressing one person.

Exodus 25 says that there is the Holy place and the Holy of Holies in the temple. In the Holy of Holies is the ark, which was made of acacia wood and overlaid with gold. This signifies the Son, who has both humanity and divinity. Inside the ark there is a golden pot, with gold signifying the divinity of the Father. This represents that the Father as the golden pot is in the Son as the ark. The golden pot as the Father contains the hidden manna, which is Christ the Son. The Bible tells us that Christ is the living bread (John 6:51). The hidden manna in the golden pot signifies that the Son is within the Father. This is an incorporation, a mutual abode.

The Holy of Holies also refers to the human spirit. The ark of the covenant, the golden pot, and the hidden manna are all contained within the human spirit. This helps us better understand what Jesus said: "I am in My Father, and you in Me, and I in you" (John 14:20). In fact, the Holy Spirit, the Comforter, is our real life, our real nature, and our real person. This is the reality!

4. The Work of Christ's Heavenly Ministry

The Lord has made this reality possible by accomplishing the judicial redemption, and through the work of His heavenly ministry, He is accomplishing His organic salvation. The organic salvation began with the disciples' experience in the upper room in Jerusalem as described in Acts 1.

Before the day of Pentecost, the disciples had received the Holy Spirit as the pneumatic Christ. They had the Holy Spirit of life within them, but the Holy Spirit as the power had not yet descended upon them. They had obtained the Lord's life and reality, but they did not have the Holy Spirit of power to testify of Christ and speak the gospel with boldness. For this, they needed the Holy Spirit to descend upon them outwardly as the Spirit of power.

On the day of His resurrection, the Lord commanded His disciples to wait for the experience of the Spirit of power, even though He had already given them the experience of the Spirit of life. They had experienced the Spirit of life inwardly, but now they had to wait to experience the Spirit of power outwardly. Although they had the life of the Lord within them, they still had to testify and work for the Lord outwardly. Their inward life was insufficient to enable them to testify and work for the Lord outwardly. They needed an external force, and they received this power on the day of Pentecost.

On the day of Jesus's resurrection, the Holy Spirit entered into the disciples to be their life, and on the day of Pentecost, the Holy Spirit descended upon them to be their strength. On the day of resurrection, they experienced the Spirit of life; on the day of Pentecost, they experienced the Holy Spirit of power. Their experience of the Holy Spirit speaks of both the inward aspect of life and the outward aspect of power.

God gives the Holy Spirit to those who believe in His Son so that they may be empowered to overcome all obstacles. One step is the giving of the Son, and the other step is the giving of the Holy Spirit. Everything accomplished in the Son is an objective truth, and everything done in believers through the working of the Holy Spirit is a subjective truth. Put more simply, all that is done in Christ is objective, and all that is done in believers through the Holy Spirit is subjective.

The experience of the Holy Spirit is different for each person, and the experience of the Spirit varies from person to person too. 1 Corinthians 12:4 says, "But there are distinctions of gifts, but the same Spirit." Verse 3 says that when believers minister by speaking in the Spirit of God, they can all say, "Jesus is Lord," exalting Jesus as Lord. But the gifts for the operation of the Spirit are diverse. The Greek word rendered "distinctions" in verse 4, and also appearing in verses 5 and 6, means "diversities, varieties, distributions." The Spirit is One, but the Spirit experienced by believers is varied.

The Spirit is not theoretical or doctrinal but is subjective truth. The Spirit as a living person is able to be experienced by each believer in a particular, specific, and varied way. In the book *Pneumatology*, Veli-Matti Kärkkäinen writes, "The experience of the Holy Spirit is as specific as the living beings who experience the Spirit, and as varied as the living beings who experience the Spirit are varied."[37]

C. Two Aspects of the Work of the Holy Spirit

Third, the work of the Holy Spirit has two aspects: the inward aspect and the outward aspect. There was a time difference between the work of the inward filling of the Holy Spirit and the work of the outpouring of the Holy Spirit. The infilling of the Holy Spirit in John 20:22 began on the day of Christ's resurrection. The Lord's promise concerning receiving the power of the Holy Spirit (Joel 2:28–29) was fulfilled on the day of Pentecost, when the outward filling of the Holy Spirit came upon the one hundred twenty (Acts 1:15; 2:1–21), which had been prophesied by the Lord.

Luke 24:49 says, "And behold, I send forth the promise of My Father upon you; but as for you, stay in the city until you

---

[37] Veli-Matti Kärkkäinen, *Pneumatology*, 4, quoted in Jürgen Moltmann, *The Source of Life: The Holy Spirit and the Theology of Life*, trans. Margaret Kohl (Minneapolis: Fortress, 1997), 56.

put on power from on high." And Acts 1:8, reads "But you shall receive power when the Holy Spirit comes upon you, and you shall be My witnesses both in Jerusalem and in all Judea and Samaria and unto the uttermost part of the earth."

The work of the Holy Spirit is different in John 20:22 from His work in Acts 2:4.[38] John 20:22 says that He breathed into them and said, "Receive the Holy Spirit." Immediately before the Lord was taken up to heaven, He referred to the Holy Spirit when He said, "Stay in the city until you put on power from on high" (Luke 24:49).

The issue of God's outpouring of His Spirit upon all flesh is our salvation through calling on the name of the Lord (Acts 2:21). God's outpouring of His Spirit is the applying of the Lord's salvation to His chosen people. To be saved is to receive the Holy Spirit. This Holy Spirit is the Lord Himself as breath (John 20:22) and living water (John 4:10, 14) for believers. To breathe Him in as the breath and to drink Him in as the living water, believers need to call on Him. Lamentations 3:55–56 indicates that the believers' calling on the Lord is their breathing.

Hymn number 1340 says, "Therefore with joy shall ye draw water, out of the wells of salvation, and in that day shall ye say, 'Praise the Lord.' Call upon His name, declare His doings among the people, make mention that His name is exalted. Cry out and shout, thou inhabitant of Zion: for great is the Holy One of Israel in the midst of Thee."[39]

To be baptized in the Spirit as mentioned in Acts 11:16 means that believers receive the Holy Spirit and have been sanctified positionally from Satan unto God to enjoy Christ.

---

[38] Watchman Nee, *CWWN*, vol. 46, 1142.
[39] Living Stream Ministry, "Therefore with Joy Shall Ye Draw Water," *Hymns*, no. 1340 (Anaheim: Living Stream Ministry, 1980), 1290, https://www.hymnal.net/en/hymn/h/1340.

The Jewish believers were baptized in the Holy Spirit on the day of Pentecost, and the Gentile believers were baptized in the Holy Spirit in the house of Cornelius. To drink of the Spirit in Ephesians 5:18 means that we believers are filled with the Spirit in our spirit, which causes us to overflow with Christ in our speaking, singing, psalming, and giving thanks to God.

We have seen the two different aspects of the Spirit. On the one hand, we believers have been baptized in the Spirit as the outpouring of the Spirit. On the other hand, we believers have been drinking the Spirit daily as if drinking water. When we constantly turn to the Spirit as the Source of living water, we are drinking Him, enjoying Him, and being filled with Him.

> The Spirit of life and the Spirit of power are two aspects of the one Spirit for our experience. We see both aspects in 1 Corinthians 12:13. On the one hand, we have all been baptized in one Spirit; on the other hand, we have all been given to drink of the one Spirit. Drinking the Spirit inwardly is essential, and being baptized in the Spirit outwardly is economical. The inward aspect of the Spirit is for life essentially, and the outward aspect of the Spirit is for ministry economically.[40]

Concerning the Spirit of life, believers should breathe Him as their breath (John 20:22). Concerning the Spirit of power, believers should be clothed with Him (Luke 24:49). The water of life requires believers to drink of it (John 7:37–39). The water of baptism requires believers to be immersed in it (Acts 1:5). These are the two aspects of the one Spirit for believers to experience (1 Cor. 12:13). The indwelling of the Spirit of life is essential to

---

[40] Witness Lee, *The Conclusion of the New Testament*, vol. 1 (Anaheim, CA: Living Stream Ministry, 1985), 1363.

their life and their living. The outpouring of the Holy Spirit of power is economical in their ministry and work.

1. The Inward Life in the Holy Spirit

The Holy Spirit was breathed into His disciples on the day of the Lord's resurrection to be the Spirit of life to them essentially speaking. The same Holy Spirit came upon the disciples on the day of Pentecost to be the Spirit of power economically speaking. The pouring out of the Spirit after Christ's ascension was the descending of the ascended Christ as the Spirit to carry out His heavenly ministry on earth to build up His church.

The same Spirit is in believers essentially and upon them economically. The word *upon* (ἐπί) in Acts 2:17 differs economically from the essential *in* (ἐν) in John 14:17. *In* is related to the intrinsic essence for life; *upon* is related to the outward element for power.

Acts 19 records twelve Ephesian believers being baptized with the baptism of John without having heard of the coming of the Holy Spirit. When Paul came to them, he asked if they had received the Holy Spirit when they believed, and they answered that they had not, but they had faith already. Through Paul's evangelism, they believed in Jesus and received the Holy Spirit. Paul did not address with them the matter of faith. In other words, faith was not the problem; the problem was that they had not received the Holy Spirit.

Genuine believers in Christ were baptized in the Holy Spirit into the Body of Christ once for all universally. In the New Testament, the Jewish believers were baptized in the Holy Spirit on the day of Pentecost. The Gentile believers were baptized in the house of Cornelius in Acts 10:44–47.

Baptism has two perspectives. When the new converts are

baptized into the water, on our side, they are baptized into the water, but on God's side, they are baptized into the Holy Spirit (Acts 1:5), into the one Body (1 Cor. 12:13), and into the Triune God (Matt. 28:19).

After receiving the Lord, many people experience the outpouring of the Holy Spirit as speaking in tongues and witnessing. When believers receive the Lord and experience the outpouring of the Holy Spirit, their faith becomes stronger. "Paul desires the Ephesians to be strengthened by means of God's Spirit (Eph. 3:16). Believers serve by the Spirit (Phil. 3:3), love by the Spirit (Col. 1:8), are sealed by the Spirit, and walk and live by the Spirit (Gal. 5:16, 25)."[41]

The fullness of the Holy Spirit, or the inner fullness, is for the growth of life. The infilling of the Holy Spirit is for the release of what is within believers. When believers follow the inward regulation, they are filled with, occupied by, and possessed by the Holy Spirit within. However, without the infilling of the Holy Spirit, it is very difficult for them to release what they have experienced in the fullness of the Holy Spirit. Even if they have many experiences of inner regulation, they will not be able to supply others with what they have experienced without the infilling of the Spirit. When they experience the fullness of the Holy Spirit, they are free to minister their inner experience of the Spirit to the saints.

The Holy Spirit indwelling believers gives the believers new strength to do God's will and to please God so that God can be their God and they can be His people. The Holy Spirit pleases God and renews believers. When believers have contact with the indwelling Holy Spirit and experience the outpouring of the Spirit, their entire being is renewed and transformed.

---

[41] Gordon D. Fee, *Paul, the Spirit, and the People of God* (Grand Rapids, MI: Baker Academic, 1996), 26.

If believers do not have a deep experience of Christ, then sometimes they may focus on gifts. There are cases where the saints do not grow in life when they pursue and follow the gifts and miracles. Those who seek external gifts often neglect to cultivate a deep understanding and to experience the Word of God and easily become arrogant.

Knowing the Lord and deeply experiencing Him is more important than seeking outward gifts and miracles. The deep spiritual things of God are discerned in the spirit, not through the understanding of the human mind, but through the enlightening of the indwelling Holy Spirit.

The inward work of the Holy Spirit within believers is for life and living. This work also yields various fruits by the supplying the life of the Holy Spirit within the believers. Galatians 5:22–23 speaks of the fruit, focusing on nine in particular: "But the fruit of the Spirit is love, joy, peace, long-suffering, kindness, goodness, faithfulness, meekness, self-control; against such things there is no law." God has given us the all-inclusive Spirit. God has not given us separate fruits of the Spirit with one called love, another called joy, and a third called peace.

Watchman Nee discussed the fruit of the Spirit:

> The outpouring of the Spirit is for testifying Christ, and the indwelling of the Spirit is for testifying Christ as well. On the one hand, the Holy Spirit within enables us to overcome. On the other hand, this Spirit within testifies that the Lord is everything to us. When the Holy Spirit is in us, we bear the fruit of the Spirit (Gal. 5:22–23), which fruit is just Christ Himself. God has not given us separate fruits of the Spirit with one called love, another called joy, and a third called endurance, etc.[42]

---

[42] Watchman Nee, *CWWN*, vol. 41, 162.

The manifestation of the filling of the Holy Spirit is a holy life, an overcoming life. Galatians 5:22–23 refers to nine fruits of the Spirit as we have seen. Matthew 5:5–9 speaks of righteousness, mercy, purity, gentleness, and peace. When we are filled with the Holy Spirit, the divine attributes are expressed. Watchman Nee affirmed this by writing the following:

> There are three chapters in the Bible that specifically speak of the Holy Spirit. They are 1 Corinthians 12 through 14. Chapters 12 and 14 are on the outpouring of the Spirit; they are related to the outward aspects of the Spirit's work. Chapter 13 is on love; it is related to the inward aspects of the Spirit's work. If we replace the phrase "the fruit of the Spirit" with the word *love*, we will see that 1 Corinthians 13 is actually speaking of the things of the Spirit. The first item of the fruit of the Spirit is love. Without love, other items, such as joy, peace, and endurance, are nothing.[43]

God has given believers His Holy Spirit: when love is needed, the fruit of the Spirit is love, and when joy is needed, the fruit of the Spirit is joy. This is always true. The fruit of the Spirit means that the divine nature of Christ is assimilated by believers through the working of the Holy Spirit and that it consequently becomes their character and inner constitution. This is the meaning of the fruits of the Holy Spirit in believers.

If Christians are filled with the Spirit within and also have the Spirit upon them, they will be empowered to do the Lord's work. However, if believers focus on the gifts, such as healing power, interpretation of tongues, and power of evangelism, they may experience the outpouring of the Spirit, but after a

---

[43] Ibid., 163.

few years at most, they will sense a lack of reality and inward emptiness because of the shortage of the growth of the divine life and a lack of the inward constitution of the divine life.

The Holy Spirit speaks to believers and anoints them to grow inwardly. The inward growth of life is absolutely a matter of being filled, but being filled requires the help of an outpouring. Faith needs a reasonable balance. When believers experience the gifts through the growth of their inner life and through their living testimony, the Lord's ministry will continually prosper.

The indwelling and infilling of the Holy Spirit are for the inner life. By the regeneration of the Spirit, believers receive the divine life. With the indwelling of the Spirit, they can be under the regulation of the divine life. With the infilling of the Holy Spirit, they will mature in life. Because everything has been done for believers, they can believe, receive, be regenerated, be filled with the Spirit, and dispense Christ to others for the building up of the church as the Body of Christ.

The Lord Jesus says, "Everything is ready. Come to the wedding feast" (Matt. 22:4). Incarnation has been accomplished, the Lord's human life has been accomplished, His all-inclusive death has been accomplished, His resurrection has been accomplished, His ascension and enthronement have been accomplished, and the indwelling of the Holy Spirit has been accomplished in believers. Believers can enjoy all the riches by believing and applying what the Lord has accomplished.

2. The Outward Power in the Holy Spirit

The coming of the Spirit was promised by God the Father. This promise had been given to the prophet Joel and is quoted by Peter in Acts 2:17-18: "And it shall be in the last days, says God, that I will pour out of My Spirit upon all flesh, and your sons and your daughters shall prophesy, and your young men shall see visions, and your old men shall dream things in dreams; and indeed upon My slaves, both men and women, I will pour out of My Spirit in those days, and they shall prophesy." These verses speak of the pouring out of the Spirit.

The pouring out of God's Spirit came from the heavens after Christ's ascension. Acts 5:14 says, "Believers were all the more being added to the Lord, multitudes of both men and women." This proves that believers who experience the power of the Holy Spirit have a solid testimony and experience.

Acts 2:33 says, "Therefore having been exalted to the right hand of God, and having received the promise of the Holy Spirit from the Father, He poured out this which you both see and hear." The exalted Christ's receiving of the promise of the Holy Spirit was the receiving of the Holy Spirit Himself. Christ was conceived of the Spirit essentially for His being in humanity, and He was anointed with the Spirit economically for His ministry among people.

After His resurrection and ascension, He is in the heavens, and He also is in His disciples' spirit essentially for their life and living. But His disciples still needed to receive the Spirit economically to carry out His heavenly ministry by the Spirit. They began to receive the economical Spirit in chapter 2 of Acts.

W. H. Griffith Thomas quoted James Welldon's illustrative account of the disciples at Pentecost:

> The descent of the Holy Spirit on the disciples at Pentecost was to them what the descent of the Holy Spirit upon our Lord at His baptism was to Him. It was their initiation into an official ministry. As in His instance, so too in theirs, it occurred on the threshold of public responsibility. After His

baptism He was no more a private man, living in
quietness and retirement, but the definite claimant
to Messiahship. And they too, after the Pentecost,
were no more timid, shrinking, reticent, half-
hearted men, no more gathered apart from society
in a small room, but bold as lions, the strenuous
advocates of the greatest of all causes, the invincible
evangelists of the world.[44]

When believers are filled with the Holy Spirit, they want
to share the gospel with others. They supply the life of Christ
to others by the leading of the indwelling Holy Spirit, who is
their power and strength. People become bold when they are
filled with the Holy Spirit. Those who were previously quiet and
shy testify just like the disciples who experienced Pentecost,
becoming bold and vigorous.

W. H. Griffith Thomas quoted Swete's account of the
Pentecostal disciples as follows:

The Peter of the Day of Pentecost is a new man,
far other than the Peter of the Passover. ... And
in courage and general understanding of the new
situation Peter was not alone; the whole company
of believers was filled with the same spirit; the
rest of the Twelve stood up with him, identifying
themselves with his words. From that day forward a
new strength, which was not their own, marked all
the sayings and deeds of the Apostolic Church. It is
in this great change of mental and spiritual attitude
rather than in the external signs of wind and fire or

---

[44] W. H. Griffith Thomas, *The Holy Spirit of God*, 42, quoting from
James Welldon, *The Revelation of the Holy Spirit* (New York: Macmillan,
1902), 153.

> in strange powers of utterance that we recognize the
> supreme miracle of the day of Pentecost.[45]

Peter and His disciples preached the gospel in the fullness of the Holy Spirit, spreading the gospel with the fullness of life and bringing people from darkness to light and from death to life. When Paul was called by God to preach the gospel, he was commanded to turn people from darkness to light and from the power of Satan to the power of God.

The authority of Satan is the kingdom of Satan. When Christians preach the gospel to sinners, they bring Satan's captives back from the power of darkness to God's light. When believers receive the fullness of the Holy Spirit inwardly and outwardly, many people are turned to the Lord.

The experience of Pentecost changed the life of Peter and the lives of all the Lord's disciples. The disciples, who experienced the infilling and outpouring of the Holy Spirit, became the invincible evangelists of the world. They also became witnesses of Christ through the essential and economical experience of the Holy Spirit.

In the Lord's resurrection, the Spirit of resurrection life is likened to breath, breathed into the disciples (John 20:22) for their inward life essentially. In the Lord's ascension, the Spirit of ascension power, poured upon the disciples, is for the disciples' ministry and move economically.

Acts 2:4 reads, "All of them were filled with the Holy Spirit and began to speak in tongues as the Spirit gave them utterance." There were one hundred twenty disciples who believed, waited, and prayed together until the promise was fulfilled (Acts 1:15). These one hundred twenty disciples received the fullness of

---

[45] Ibid., quoting Henry Barclay Swete, *The Holy Spirit in the New Testament* (Eugene: Wipf and Stock, 1998), 76.

the Holy Spirit by believing in the Lord's promise and praying on the day of Pentecost (Acts 2:4). At another time, Christ appeared to more than five hundred saints at one time (1 Cor. 15:6).

Before His death, the Lord was in the flesh and His presence was visible. After His resurrection, the Lord became the Spirit and His presence was invisible. During the forty days after His resurrection, Jesus came, though the doors were shut, and stood in the midst of His disciples and said, "Peace be to you" (John 20:26).

In fact, on the morning of His resurrection, before the Lord ascended to the heavens, He appeared to Mary Magdalene and said to her, "Do not touch Me, for I have not yet ascended to the Father." He continued, saying, "I ascend to My Father" (John 20:17).

In the evening of the same day, the Lord again appeared to the disciples and said, "Touch Me and see" (Luke 24:39). By this time, the Lord was able to allow human beings to touch Him. This reveals that before this time He had already ascended to the heavens and offered to God the freshness of His resurrection.

After His resurrection, His appearances were more precious than His visible presence. The Lord trained His disciples to realize, enjoy, and practice His invisible presence as a reality. In His resurrection, this dear presence of His was just the Spirit, whom He had breathed into them and who would be with them all the time.

On the day of Pentecost, ten days after the ascension, the disciples were all clothed with and filled with the Holy Spirit. Because they were all filled with the resurrected Christ, the indwelling Spirit as the invisible One, they were able to be together for ten days and pray together in one accord. On the day of Pentecost, three thousand people received the Holy

Spirit and were baptized. Acts 2:42 says that these individuals continued steadfastly in the teaching and the fellowship of the apostles, in the breaking of bread, and in their prayers.

D. The Continual Anointing and Operating of the Spirit

Fourth, the anointing is a feeling rather than something clearly spoken. It may seem to be a spoken word as well as a feeling, but it can never be a clearly and definitely spoken sentence. When we live in the presence of the Lord and have fellowship with Him, the Holy Spirit unveils our feeling. The anointing is inward and subjective rather than outward and objective.

If our spiritual life is normal, we will feel the anointing in a spontaneous way. The anointing is constant, not coincidental. The Holy Spirit grants us this feeling in our daily life. "The anointing of the Holy Spirit gives the believers' spirit a certain feeling when it is applied. When the intuition becomes aware of this feeling, it knows what the Holy Spirit is speaking."[46]

The anointing comes from the Holy Spirit. If we obey the teaching of the anointing constantly, we can constantly experience the anointing and live in the mingled spirit. It is not difficult to experience the anointing and obey its teachings, because it is characteristically constant and spontaneous. Spontaneous means that we automatically have the anointing, and constant means that it is always available. The main purpose of experiencing the anointing is that we touch God Himself and have His presence.

When we believers pass through the veil of the flesh and live in the presence of God, we have fellowship with God in the Holy of Holies, the Spirit. At this time, we experience the anointing

---

[46] Watchman Nee, *The Spiritual Man (2)*, 295.

and have His presence. First John 2:27 says, "And as for you, the anointing which you have received from Him abides in you, and you have no need that anyone teach you; but as His anointing teaches you concerning all things and is true and is not a lie, and even as it has taught you, abide in Him."

The Holy Spirit who dwells in the believers' spirits is moving and acting all the time. This working, moving, acting, or motion of the Holy Spirit is the anointing. Through this anointing, believers are sanctified and deified. Those who live and act according to the anointing are those who live according to the guidance of the Holy Spirit.

> The anointing will teach the believer "concerning all things." He will not leave him or allow him to make his own choice. Everyone who wants to walk according to the spirit must realize this. Our responsibility is nothing else but to be taught. We do not need to decide on our own way; actually, we cannot decide anyway. Anything apart from the leading of the anointing is just our own action.[47]

Anointing originally refers to anointing with oil. The way the Holy Spirit teaches, works, and speaks to believers is through the human spirit, within which He works quietly so that they sense something with their intuition. When believers are sensitive to the anointing, they have more time with the Lord and come to know Him and enjoy Him. The anointing causes believers to grow in faith. As they spend more time with the Lord, they grow more.

Believers should be renewed day by day in the Holy Spirit for their growth in life and to gain maturity. To do this, believers need to seek the infilling of the Holy Spirit in both aspects:

---

[47] Ibid.

essentially and economically. But realistically, to Christians, the Holy Spirit is unreal. They regard Him as a mere influence, an influence for good no doubt.

The Corinthian Christians' problem was not that they lacked the indwelling Holy Spirit, but that they lacked the knowledge of the presence of the indwelling Spirit, the pneumatic Christ. They did not realize the greatness of the One who indwelt them. Paul wrote to them: "Do you not know that you are the temple of God and that the Spirit of God dwells in you?" This question was both a question about their nonspiritual state and an answer at the same time. Their cure was simply to know who the One who dwelled in them really was.

Although invisible to the eyes of humankind, the Holy Spirit is the One who works in the spirit of His believers. If believers do not know how to turn to the spirit, then their spiritual life is inconsistent. When believers turn to the spirit, they experience the divine anointing, that is, the work of the indwelling Holy Spirit, which brings them into the divine Trinity, especially into the person of Christ (1 John 2:27). The fresh anointing renews believers and enables them to grow in faith.

When believers walk according to the spirit, set their mind on the spirit, and live according to the spirit of life, they are freed from sin and live a normal Christian life. Believers live a new life when they are trained to turn to their spirit, that is, their *conscience* (gut feeling) and *intuition* (spontaneous feeling), and to *fellowship* (pray) with the Lord every day. These three are the parts of the spirit. The moment believers turn to the spirit, touch the Lord, and remain in the spirit, they spontaneously experience the killing power to their thoughts, imaginations, and desires of their sinful nature.

1. The Believer's Growth in Life by Being Nourished

The anointing of the indwelling Holy Spirit causes believers to grow in the divine life. When believers receive the fresh anointing of the Spirit, their inner being is saturated with the Spirit and is renewed. By this fresh anointing day after day, their life is renewed; and by being renewed, they are sanctified; and by being sanctified, they are united with God in Christ and deified in life. This is an organic union, a union of life, between believers and God in Christ.

In regard to the indwelling of the Spirit, Sinclair B. Ferguson says, "The analogy we are offered is that the mutual indwelling of Christ and the believer is shaped according to the pattern of inner-trinitarian relationships. Just as there is a mutual indwelling of Father and Son revealed by the Spirit, so by the indwelling of the same Spirit, Christ and the believer are united (John 14:20)."[48]

Growth comes from the fresh anointing and by being nourished daily. To be nourished with Christ to grow in life is what His people need today, and this is the mark of God's economy. Through nourishment, we grow, and through growth, we are fitted together with one another. Furthermore, we are knit together and built up.

Ephesians 4:13 says, "Until we all arrive at the oneness of the faith and of the full knowledge of the Son of God, at a full-grown man, at the measure of the stature of the fullness of Christ." The full knowledge of the Son of God is the understanding of the revelation concerning the Son of God for the believers' experience. The more that believers grow in life, the more they will adhere to the faith and understand Christ, and the more they will drop every trivial and vile doctrinal concept that

---

[48] Sinclair B. Ferguson, *The Holy Spirit*, 176.

causes division. Then they will come to a real oneness. In other words, they will be perfected to be full-grown with the stature of the fullness of Christ.

The Son of God refers to the person of the Lord who is life. Christ imparts life to His believers, members of His Body, so that they may have gifts to function. The Lord shepherds His flock by nourishing them and cherishing them so that they may become mature in the divine life (Eph. 5:29). Peter was a simple fisherman. God often chooses simple people. D. L. Moody was a shoe salesman when he was saved, but he became a great evangelist. God uses people who simply convey the Word of divine life.

First Peter 2:2–3 says, "As newborn babes, long for the guileless milk of the word in order that by it you may grow unto salvation. If you have tasted that the Lord is good." After new believers are born with new life in Christ, they should rely on the milk of the Word to grow until they reach the full enjoyment of salvation.

When D. L. Moody was preaching the gospel, he caused many people to shed tears: "Mr. Moody took charge, and it seemed as though the Spirit of the Lord came down upon these men [those who sought to convert] with great power. They came forward to the altar—twenty, thirty, forty at a time. We closed the meeting and began inquiry work. Moody had the platform, and God used him wonderfully. The audience melted, and we saw strong men in tears."[49] Moody was a person who was always ready to preach the gospel in his spirit.

The Lord said to Peter, "Feed My lambs" (John 21:15). The second time, the Lord told him, "Shepherd My sheep" (v. 16). Then He said a third time, "Feed My sheep" (v. 17). The Lord

---

[49] W. R. Moody, *The Life of Dwight L. Moody* (Westwood, NJ: Barbour and Company, 1985), 78.

did not tell Peter to teach or instruct, or even to edify, but just to feed. Believers' love for the Lord should issue in the feeding of His lambs. Finally, the Lord Jesus gave Peter one additional Word: "Follow Me" (vv. 19, 22).

The Lord Jesus is in the spirit of the believers. We believers follow the Lord by eating, drinking, and enjoying the Lord's words in our spirit. And we should go to the new believers and feed them. To feed and nurture them is to make them grow, and to make them grow is to build them up as members of Christ's Body.

The Lord is in us and is one spirit with us (1 Cor. 6:17). Dwelling in us, the Lord is waiting for us to be renewed and transformed into His image by the resurrection life. We should be renewed in our mind, emotion, and will in order to overcome all negative things and to live a life of doing the will of the Lord. Because the mind is the guiding part of the soul, it is important that our mind be renewed. When our mind is renewed, our spirit will be released.

Watchman Nee emphasized the breaking of the outer man:

> God has to break the outer man before He can use the inner man. He has to break our love before He can use our love to love the brothers. If the outer man is not broken, we are still doing our own things, taking our own way, and loving our own preferences. God must first break our outer man before He can use our "broken" love to love the brothers and before our love can be expanded. Once the outer man is broken, the inner man is released. The inner man must love, but it must love through the outer man. If the outer man has things in its hands, the inner man will have nothing to work through.[50]

---

[50] Watchman Nee, *The Breaking of the Outer Man and the Release of the Spirit* (Anaheim: Living Stream Ministry, 1997), 34.

When the outer self is broken and our inner person is released, we will spontaneously touch the Spirit and receive the anointing. When we live by the spirit and walk by the spirit, we shall by no means fulfill the lust of the flesh. Whenever we walk by the spirit, we have the Lord's leading, even in such ordinary matters as the way we converse with others. However, whenever we live according to the flesh, we will not only become independent from God, but also we will be stubborn, occupied, and unable to cooperate with others.

Watchman Nee continued, writing:

> Our will is strong. It is not only strong; it is also stubborn. When our inner man needs the will, it cannot find it, because our will has been moving too independently and has too many things in its hands. God has to give us a heavy blow; He has to smash our will and humble us so much that we are forced to say, with our face in the dust, "Lord, I dare not think. I dare not ask. I dare not decide. I need You in everything." We must be so smitten that our will can no longer act independently. Only then can the inner man take hold of the will and use it.[51]

Growth in life is achieved when the indwelling Christ spreads from our spirit into our soul so that He may saturate, possess, and occupy our inward parts (Eph. 3:17; Heb. 8:10). As a result, we will have a real increase in Christ as our nourishment and life supply (Heb. 4:16). We cannot help the saints simply by teaching them. Neither scolding nor condemnation helps them. In order to open the way for Christ to increase in the saints, we should minister Christ to the converts and feed them with Christ by dispensing Christ.

---

[51] Ibid., 34–35.

2. Renewal and Transformation by the Spiritual Food

The Lord's work is to enable us to eat and enjoy the Lord. The way for us to increase in Christ is to eat and digest Him (John 6:51–57). Digestion is what allows the food eaten to have a free path inside our body so that it can be assimilated into the blood vessels, organs, and fibers of the body. Therefore, we should eat Christ by pray-reading the Word (Eph. 6:17–18).

In order to digest Christ as the Word of God, we need to open our entire being to Him. The basic principle of pray-reading is to exercise the spirit, release the spirit, and touch the spirit. When we read the Bible, we receive God's Word into our mind. When we pray-read the Bible verses, we receive the Word of God deep in our spirit.

When we do this, we digest Him by allowing Him to have passage into our being. When we eat the Word of God and pray, we assimilate spiritual food. As a result, Christ increases in us, saturates us, possesses us, and occupies us. As we grow in life, we become worthy, useful, and functioning members of the body. Living, functioning members of the Body of Christ are not slothful. Instead, we are diligent.

When the saints enjoy the Lord, they have true growth in life, which takes place in their spirit. When they are in the spirit, they can enjoy the Word of the Lord and, in so doing, be made new. To grow in life is to achieve growth in Christ. To grow in Christ is the increase of Christ, the addition of Christ. As Christ increases in us, our mind is renewed, filled, and saturated with the Lord.

The Lord infuses us with His divine life, which is always new, never old, and is eternal. We are renewed day by day by putting off the old nature and living out the new life of the new creation. We in the old creation need to be renewed by allowing God to daily infuse His attributes into our inward being.

The Holy Spirit is the divine person who washes us and renews us with the divine life, making us a new creation with the divine element. Washing and renewing are matters of life; they are part of the process of growth. It is possible to grow with the life of God. Therefore, we grow into Christ and walk in newness of life. This is certainly a wonderful experience as we enjoy Christ as our new life.

The believers' secret is that in their spirit dwells the uncreated divine Spirit, who imparts the divine life into the *tripartite human being*.[52] Believers are those who have the life of Christ and who live by the indwelling Holy Spirit. Madame Guyon, who experienced the indwelling Spirit deep within her, stated the following:

> A constant practice of turning inward, there touching the Lord's gracious anointing. With this touch He draws to Himself. Eventually, His Life and Spirit—dwelling deep within you—get the upper hand of your external nature. After all, your natural man is an inferior part of you. The Lord, who dwells supreme in the innermost portions of your being, is the higher portion of you. This inferior portion, this natural man, comes under subjection. Without resistance, without striving and without struggle, the external weaknesses are cared for.[53]

---

[52] The tripartite human being is body, soul, and spirit. God is triune; humankind is tripartite. In Romans 8, we are told that the mind is set on the spirit; the mind becomes life, and eventually life is given even to the mortal body.

[53] Madame Jeanne Guyon, *Union with God* (Augusta, ME: Christian Books, 1981), 28–29.

The indwelling work of the Holy Spirit anoints believers, saturating them and permeating them from within, and leads them to Christ. Believers need to know that the indwelling Spirit needs their cooperation. With this cooperation, the Lord continually works in them and anoints them. The anointing is the work of the indwelling Holy Spirit, who brings believers into the reality of the divine Trinity, especially into the person of Christ (1 John 2:27). Again, believers are those who live according to the spirit.

The Holy Spirit dwells in believers as the seal, guarantee, and Comforter, guiding them into all reality, teaching them all things, bringing them into union with Christ, fellowshipping with Christ, interceding for them, and reminding them of the Word of God.

Ephesians 4:30 says, "Do not grieve the Holy Spirit of God, in whom you were sealed unto the day of redemption." When believers are sealed by the Spirit, they are saved. The Spirit, as the seal in the believers, seals them continually with the element of God so that they may be transformed in nature until their bodies are completely transfigured and redeemed.[54]

The Spirit's indwelling of believers is a reality. Whenever they call on the name of the Lord, the indwelling Spirit becomes real to them. Paul exhorts believers to pray without ceasing (1 Thess. 5:17). Just as a person's physical existence is sustained by breathing, likewise, a believer's spiritual existence is sustained by breathing. The way to breathe spiritually is to pray and to call on the name of the Lord. For a proper spiritual life, a believer should pray, call on the Lord, and live according to the spirit.

Christians live primarily according to their own nature, culture, ethical practices, or habits. Many do not understand how they can live according to the spirit. There is a truth about

---

[54] Witness Lee, *Holy Bible Recovery Version*, Ephesians 4:30, footnote 5.

walking according to the spirit, but it is not enough to know this truth. Christians should practice living according to the spirit.

Christians who desire to live in Christ should do everything according to the spirit. When they do not live by the spirit, they are living according to the flesh and living according to the soul. When believers walk according to the spirit, set their mind on the spirit, and live according to the Spirit of life, they are freed from sin and live in Christ as the person in their spirit.

By the indwelling of the Holy Spirit, more of the essence and element of God are added and increased within His believers, which shapes them into the image of the firstborn Son of God. The Triune God is embodied in Christ and realized as the Spirit. Both the embodiment and reality of God indwell believers and work within them to become the content of their entire being. Because of the indwelling Holy Spirit, believers become God's dwelling place and become one spirit with God.

3. Setting the Mind on the Spirit in Our Daily Living

First Corinthians 6:17 says, "He who is joined to the Lord is one spirit." This refers to the organic union of believers with the Lord through faith in Him (John 3:15–16). Such a union with the resurrected Lord can only occur in the spirit. When believers turn to the spirit, exercise the spirit, and live according to the spirit, the law of the Spirit of life in their own spirit will free them from their sin and the sinful nature.

The secret of being free from sin and death is to set their mind on the spirit and live in their spirit according to the law of the Spirit of life. No matter how complicated and difficult the situation may be, if the mind is set on the spirit, then they will have life and peace (Rom. 8:6).

Walking according to the spirit is contrasted with walking according to the flesh. If believers do not walk according to the spirit, they walk according to the flesh. Sometimes they may walk according to the spirit, and sometimes they may walk according to the flesh. However, believers should learn to live not according to the soul.

Formerly the soul was our person, but today our person is our regenerated spirit indwelt by Christ. When we live in the soul, we are living in the self and are involved with Satan, sin, and the flesh. When we deny the soul, and we live according to the spirit, we are delivered from Satan, sin, the flesh, and the self.

When we live according to our conscience and fellowship and intuition, we will continue to grow in the spirit, and the divine life will be expanded in us. "Continue growing. Let your spirit be enlarged to greater and greater degrees. God can enlarge your spirit daily. You will be expanded in Him like the torrent. Let yourself be carried further and further into the sea."[55]

The normal experience of Christ is to live according to our spirit. "When one sets out to move in the inward way, be sure that his views will, necessarily, be self-directed and they will be complex. This is as it should be. But they will eventually become simple and more centered in the spirit."[56] When we are in spirit, we will realize what God is operating in us.

Philippians 2:13 says, "For it is God who operates in you both the willing and the working for His good pleasure." It is not that the believers by themselves carry out the work, but that God operates in them to do it.

---

[55] Jeanne Guyon, *Spiritual Torrents* (Jacksonville, FL: The SeedSowers, 1994), 74.
[56] Jeanne Guyon, *Final Steps in Christian Maturity* (Jacksonville, FL: SeedSowers, 1915), 30.

When the Spirit works, that is Christ working, and when Christ works, that is God working. Therefore, by setting our minds on the spirit, we become one with the Lord so that He can continue to expand in our entire being. "You can experience God in ever-increasing ways. Your soul's own desires, as good as they may be, also stand in the way of letting this expansion happen. The part that stands in the way is the part that must die—not your unique personality. You must let go of your old nature so that you might lose yourself more deeply in God. Your ability to grow in Him is limitless."[57]

In summary, the human spirit is the key to our Christian life, and it is God's dwelling place on the earth. In Chapter 1, we learned that Christ as the Spirit dwells in the human spirit.

First, we saw that humans are made up of three parts: spirit, soul, and body, and that the human spirit is the organ through which God enters. However, the human spirit is dead because of sin and is separated from God.

Second, the incarnation of Christ came to the earth as the first Comforter, and through Christ's death and resurrection, the pneumatic Christ as the second Comforter has entered into our spirit.

Third, we learned that through the inward work of the Holy Spirit, we experience the growth of life, and have the increase of the testimony of Christ and the spread of the gospel through the outpouring work of the Spirit.

Fourth, the Spirit is the living God who dwells within us believers, and He speaks to us and becomes us through His constant anointing and inward constituting work. Through this inward growth, we express and live out Christ, and Christ reigns in our Christian life.

---

[57] Jeanne Guyon, *Spiritual Torrents*, 75.

CHAPTER 2
Four Primary Issues Concerning the Holy Spirit

CHAPTER 2 ADDRESSES FOUR MAIN ISSUES CONCERNING THE Holy Spirit, and it consists of four parts. The first is the distinction between the influence of the Spirit and the person of the Spirit for the Christian life. The issue is that one side claims that the Holy Spirit is God's empowering influence for the believer's Christian life, and the other side contends that the Holy Spirit is a living person who works within the believers throughout their Christian life.

A second issue has been raised by another group of people who have a different view of the Spirit's work. One group insists that the Holy Spirit was in people in the Old Testament and that in the New Testament, the Holy Spirit is upon human beings. The other group emphasizes that in the Old Testament the Spirit came upon people, but in the New Testament the Spirit dwells in believers and upon believers.

Third, a claim has been made that there was no difference in the work of the Holy Spirit in John the Baptist and in the Lord Jesus. People on the other side of this argument declare that the Lord Jesus's ministry was different from John the Baptist's. One scholar, James D. G. Dunn, highlighted, "John's water baptism is only a shadow and symbol of the Christ's Spirit baptism. The contrast between the two baptisms is the contrast between

John and Jesus—the antithesis of preparation and fulfillment, of shadow and substance."[58]

Fourth, some contend that in John 20:22, after Jesus's resurrection, when He breathed into His disciples and said to them, "Receive the Holy Spirit," this was merely symbolic and representative of John's literary and theological leanings.[59] Therefore, it is argued that what the early disciples experienced at Easter should not be viewed as a pattern for post-Pentecostal believers today.[60]

People on the other side of this argument assert that after Jesus's resurrection, He breathed His life into His disciples in John 20:22 and that on the day of Pentecost, His disciples received the power of the Holy Spirit (Acts 1–2). Let us take a look at these four primary issues in the shining light of the truth and by turning to other scholars to address them in more detail.

A. The Difference Between Life and Power in the Spirit

First is the difference between an influence of the Spirit and the person of the Spirit for the believer's Christian life. One group asserts that the Holy Spirit is the influence and the power of God who works upon the believers. The other group contends that the Holy Spirit is the person of Christ, who works from within the believers throughout their entire Christian life.

We all need to know these two aspects of the Spirit as an influence and as the person for the Christian life. The strong power of the Holy Spirit is needed for powerful gospel preaching and for signs and wonders. For the daily life and inner growth

---

[58] James D. G. Dunn, *Baptism in the Holy Spirit* (London: SCM, 1970), 19.
[59] Archie Hui, "The Pneumatology of Watchman Nee: A New Testament Perspective," *Evangelical Quarterly* 75, no. 4 (2003): 19–23, 29.
[60] Ibid., 24.

of believers, we should have daily contact with the Lord as a living person.

For normal Christians, Ephesians 4:30 says, "Do not grieve the Holy Spirit of God, in whom you were sealed unto the day of redemption." This means that the Holy Spirit is a living person with feelings who dwells within believers[61] and continually seals them with the divine elements of God for their growth and maturity.

When believers take Christ as their person for their Christian life, their spirit will not be merely an organ to contact God but will also be God's dwelling place and the real person to express God. When Christ is the believer's person, He will renew their mind, emotion, and will. He will make His home in their heart, and will become their intrinsic constitution and their outward and inward power. When Christ is the believer's person, then that person can declare, "It is no longer I who live, but it is Christ who lives in me" (Gal. 2:20).

If we receive Christ as our person, then Christ will be our life and will grow in our inner being. Concerning Christ as the believers' life, Ron Kangas articulated, "It is impossible to separate our life from our person, for our life is actually we ourselves. If we did not have life, we would cease to exist. To say that Christ is our life is actually to say that He has become subjective to us to such an extent that He has been wrought into our being."[62]

If we exercise our spirit, then Christ will have the opportunity to live in us as our person. He will continuously be our person and our life supply. We will grow in His divine life so that we

---

[61] Watchman Nee, *The Spiritual Man (2)* (Anaheim: Living Stream Ministry, 1992), 224.

[62] Ron Kangas, "Pneumatic Christ," *Affirmation & Critique* 2, no. 4 (October 1997), 6.

may live because of Him (John 6:57). When He becomes our life and our person, He will be freely expressed through us.

The Lord Jesus Christ wants to come into our being to become our person as well as our life so that we may be His expression. By uniting with the Lord, we possess not only humanity, but also Christ's divine life and nature. Christ is not only our life, our person, but also our power. We have not only the divine life and nature within us, but also divine power and expression in our ministry. This divine power and expression primarily come from our inward constitution rather than from power.

After Christ's ascension on the day of Pentecost, the Lord poured out the Holy Spirit from heaven upon the disciples as power. This pouring out was like a torrent. In this way, all the disciples were empowered. Before the day of Pentecost, the disciples had spent ten days praying together. They had already received the Holy Spirit as their life on the day of Christ's resurrection.

On the day of Pentecost, the one hundred twenty disciples had been praying together with one accord for ten days to carry out God's move on the earth. When the Spirit came down upon them, they stood up to speak to the people, and three thousand were brought under conviction. The disciples had power in their preaching.

We need to see that we have the Spirit of life within us and the Spirit of power upon us. The experience of life on the day of resurrection and of power on the day of Pentecost were not given only once: believers continually experience the same life and same power everywhere the gospel is preached. If the gospel is preached according to God's will, people will receive life from it.

The Spirit of life is powerful. If we try to focus on the

visible power of the Spirit and His work, we may miss the inner anointing of the Holy Spirit. However, when we focus more on the inner growth of life, we Christians will experience and enjoy Christ, and be empowered in Christ to do all things.

Philippians 4:12-13 says, "I know also how to be abased, and I know how to abound; in everything and in all things, I have learned the secret both to be filled and to hunger, both to abound and to lack. I am able to do all things in Him who empowers me." In all our circumstances and conditions, Christ as the power of God enables us to suffer, to bear burdens, and to stand firm in unwavering faith.

1.   The Spirit Dwelling in the Deepest Part of Our Being

The universe is made up of heaven and earth, but God does not make heaven His dwelling place. The Bible shows that all of God's work is to gain His people as God's dwelling place. Also, God does not regard the earth as a dwelling place for people.

God mingled Himself with His believers in order to be one with them and to dwell in them. For both God and His believers, the real abode of the universe is neither heaven nor earth, much less a physical house. Rather, it is a place of mutual union between God and His believers. God's dwelling place is the human spirit. To dwell in the human spirit, God went through many processes in order to enter into His believers.

The dwelling place of the Holy Spirit is in the human spirit.

> The Holy Spirit indwelling man's spirit is a very important thing. If a believer does not know that the dwelling place of the Holy Spirit is in the deepest part of his whole being, which is deeper than his mind, emotion, and will, he will surely seek the guidance of the Holy Spirit in his mind, emotion,

and will. If we understand this, then we will know that we were deceived before and were wrong in looking outward, outside the spirit in the soul, or inside or outside the body for guidance. The Holy Spirit is indeed dwelling in the deepest part of our being.[63]

Since there was a lack of revelation concerning the Holy Spirit in the seventeenth century, the King James Version of the Bible did not use the personal pronoun *Himself* when referring to the Holy Spirit in Romans 8; instead, it used the neuter pronoun *itself* (vv. 16, 26).

It was not until a century ago, when the church began to realize that the Holy Spirit is a person, that the neuter pronoun was changed to a personal pronoun. A. W. Tozer wrote, "He is a Person. Put that down in capital letters—that the Holy Spirit is not only a Being having another mode of existence, but He is Himself a Person, with all the qualities and powers of personality."[64]

The Spirit is the essence of the personality of the Trinity. Therefore, "this Spirit of the divine life is now to be in us, in the deepest sense of the word—the essence of our lives, the root of our personalities, the very life of our being. He is one with us, dwelling in us, even as the Father in the Son and the Son in the Father."[65] The Spirit operates within believers and increases the divine element in their soul, their inner being.

We experience Christ as life in the deepest part. When we enter into the Holy of Holies, we enter fully into the deepest

---

[63] Watchman Nee, *The Spiritual Man (2)*, 228.

[64] A. W. Tozer, *How to Be Filled with the Holy Spirit* (Chicago: Moody, 2016), 10.

[65] Andrew Murray, *The Spirit of Christ* (New Kensington, PA: Whitaker House, 1984), 90.

part. We touch Christ in the Holy of Holies, our spirit, and are in His presence. Whatever we experience in the Holy of Holies, our spirit, we experience Christ as the Spirit. Through our conscience, through fellowship with the Lord, and through the insight of intuition, we can contact God, enjoy God, and become one with God.

All believers are saved by their faith, but for many people, their daily life is still the same as before they believed. Although their life is the new life, their nature has not yet changed, so they live and walk according to their own concepts, habits, and knowledge. If they knew the indwelling Holy Spirit's work within them, they would be able to contact Him, touch Him, and experience Him so that they may grow in the divine life.

The Lord Jesus showed Nicodemus that what he needed was not outward teachings but an inward change of life. When we believers know Christ and experience Him, we will grow into Him and be filled with Him.

In order for believers to be spiritual, they should take Christ as their person. In John 6:57, the Lord said, "As the living Father has sent Me and I live because of the Father, so he who eats Me, he also shall live because of Me." Just as the Lord Jesus did not live because of Himself but because of the Father, His believers should not live because of themselves but because of the Lord.

The Lord took the Father as His person; likewise, Christians should take the Lord as their person. Instead of trying to be patient, loving, humble, moral, or spiritual, they should simply take Christ as their person. Christ lives in our spirit, and our spirit is our person because Christ dwells in our spirit. Hence, whatever we do, through the cross, by the spirit, is for living out Christ.

Galatians 2:20 speaks of the life of the apostle Paul. "It is no longer I who live, but it is Christ who lives in me." If believers take Christ as their person instead of trying to be spiritual by their own effort, they will be genuinely living Christ as their person.

Believers are members of the Body of Christ, wherein there is not only divine life, but also a divine person, namely, Christ. Believers should experience Christ not only as their life, but also—and much more—as their person. All divine and spiritual riches are in the person of Christ, who is the indwelling Spirit.

2. The Inward Filling and the Outpouring of the Spirit

The other aspect of the Holy Spirit is God's empowering presence, which influences the experience of believers. Christ is the One who empowers believers. In Philippians 4:13 Paul says, "I can do all things in Him who empowers me." If Christians experience the Holy Spirit upon them, then they have power and are gifted. Acts 1:5 says, "For John baptized with water, but you shall be baptized in the Holy Spirit."

To be baptized in the Holy Spirit means to be not only filled outwardly with the Spirit, but also absolutely infilled with the Spirit. Inwardly they are already filled with the Spirit and are ready to be baptized in the name of Jesus, and outwardly they are baptized in the name of Jesus by the Spirit.

In this way, Christians have life, have power, and have a gift. "Inwardly we need to be filled with the Holy Spirit, and outwardly we need power and gift. If we do not have power and gift, we are not complete in the experience of the Holy Spirit."[66]

Peter was filled with the Holy Spirit, and God worked through him to heal a lame man and caused him to walk (Acts 3:1–10). Paul came to Ephesus and testified of Christ to the Ephesians, and they received the Holy Spirit. They spoke in tongues, and they prophesied (Acts 19:1–7).

---

[66] Witness Lee, *CWWL*, 1963, vol. 3, 372.

The experience of the Ephesian believers was like the experience of the Samaritan believers (8:4–13). Twelve of the early Ephesian believers were like the Samaritan believers who believed in the Lord and were saved, but those people did not experience the outward filling of the Holy Spirit. When Paul came and laid hands on them, they received the outpouring of the Holy Spirit. At that time, they spoke in tongues and prophesied.

In the New Testament, prophesying means speaking for Christ and speaking forth Christ. When a person repents for the forgiveness of his sins, he receives the Holy Spirit. Furthermore, when he thoroughly repents and turns to the Lord, he receives the outpouring of the Holy Spirit.

In Charles G. Finney's testimony, after his thorough repenting, he received a mighty baptism of the Holy Spirit:

> I received a mighty baptism of the Holy Spirit. Without any expectation of it, without ever having the thought in my mind that there was any such thing for me, without any memory of ever hearing the thing mentioned by any person in the world, the Holy Spirit descended upon me in a manner that seemed to go through me, body, and soul. I could feel the impression, like a wave of electricity, going through and through me. Indeed, it seemed to come in waves of liquid love, for I could not express it in any other way.[67]

By such a thorough repentance, Finney knew that the Holy Spirit first cleansed his inward parts with the blood of Jesus, and then he experienced the outpouring power of the Holy

---

[67] Charles G. Finney, *The Autobiography of Charles G. Finney* (Bloomington, MN: Bethany House, 1977), 21.

Spirit. In this regard, Witness Lee testified that the outward filling is for the manifestation of gifts and for power. "With the outpouring there is the manifestation of the gifts. However, the real function of the gifts depends upon the growth in life, which results from the infilling of the Spirit. If we do not have the infilling, we will not have the growth in life and consequently will not have the proper function."[68]

Without thorough repentance by way of the Holy Spirit, believers doubt that the Lord is indwelling them. With only an outward manifestation, we cannot say that believers are filled with the Holy Spirit and thereby experience growth in life.

Without the continual anointing within, such believers are like the Corinthian believers, who had the outward manifestation of gifts, but no inward receipt of growth in life or the fullness of the Spirit. These were carnal believers. "They were Christians, in Christ, but instead of being spiritual Christians, they were carnal. I have fed you with milk, and not with meat, for hitherto ye were not able to bear it, neither yet are ye able, for ye are yet carnal."[69]

The Corinthian believers were infants in the experience of Christ and were frustrated, unable to enter into the full enjoyment of Christ, because they were soulish and fleshly. Thus, they needed growth in life (1 Cor. 3:1–3). Some among them who were not fleshly were soulish, living out their natural life (2:14). Even though what they did may not have been evil or sinful, it was soulish and natural.

The jealousy and strife among the Corinthian believers showed that they walked according to the flesh and not according to the infilling of the Spirit. Hence, they were not

---

[68] Witness Lee, *CWWL*, 1963, vol. 4, 307.
[69] Andrew Murray, *The Master's Indwelling* (Monee, IL: New Christian Classics Library, 2018), 9.

spiritual but fleshly, and they walked not according to the indwelling Spirit but according to the manner of the flesh.

Some Christians emphasize the power of the Holy Spirit, but they are poor in the knowledge of what the Holy Spirit really desires. Believers should not be childish. In order to grow unto maturity, they need to eat solid food (Heb. 5:14; Col. 1:28). There are spiritual teeth that can chew such solid food, and there are spiritual stomachs that can digest such words. The work of the indwelling Holy Spirit helps believers to eat and digest solid food and to grow unto the stature of the fullness of Christ (Eph. 4:13).

We believers have been Christians for a long time but still cannot eat solid food. Although we have been saved, our life, personality, and actions may still be the same as those of unbelievers, that is, still natural people. We may fight for our own interests. However, once the resurrection life is experienced, we will not fight for our own interests because we will know that our gain comes from our loss. This is not a doctrine. This is altogether a matter of our experience.

If no death, no life! John 12:24 says, "Unless the grain of wheat falls into the ground and dies, it abides alone; but if it dies, it bears much fruit." When we experience the living Word of God, we will experience the reality of resurrection. In resurrection, to die is to live, and to reject is to gain.

Today the Spirit is the Spirit of resurrection, the indwelling Spirit, the Spirit living within us. His presence with us is inward, and the strength, illumination, guidance, and comfort that He gives are inward. All that He gives us and does for us comes from within. John 6 says that the Spirit enters into us through the Word of the Lord, and chapter 7 says that the Spirit as the Spirit of resurrection enters into us.

When we receive the Word of God, the Spirit comes into us.

When the Spirit comes into us, we are resurrected and made alive. Ephesians 2 says that God made us alive when we were dead in our offenses and sins. We are made alive because the Spirit of resurrection in John 7 has entered into us.

The Spirit enters into us through the Word of God. Moreover, the Spirit who enters into us is the Spirit of resurrection, and as such, He enlivens our deadened spirit. The Spirit not only enlivens our spirit, but also daily supplies us with the divine life so that we may grow up into Christ in all things.

B. The Different Work of the Spirit in the Old and New Testaments

Second is an issue that has been raised by another group of people who have a different view of the Spirit's work, namely, that the Holy Spirit was in people in the Old Testament, whereas in the New Testament, the Holy Spirit is upon believers.

One article refers to three Old Testament verses discussing the Spirit's relationship with human beings: Genesis 41:38 (Joseph), Numbers 27:18 (Joshua), and Daniel 5:11 (Daniel). It contends that these verses prove that the Old Testament also speaks of the Spirit dwelling in human beings.[70]

The other group emphasizes that in the Old Testament, the Spirit came upon people, but in the New Testament, the Spirit dwells in human beings and upon them.

Even though the Spirit of God worked with power in the Old Testament, the Spirit of God could not dwell in human beings because of their fallen human nature, since Adam's sin had not yet been dealt with. After the Lord Jesus was crucified,

---

[70] Archie Hui, "The Pneumatology of Watchman Nee," 10.

and He destroyed Satan's work by His death and resurrection, then the Holy Spirit could enter into people.

There is a considerable difference between the Old Testament and the New Testament. Concerning the Spirit of God's working upon certain individuals in the Old Testament, Don Stewart wrote the following:

> "The Spirit of the Lord came upon, or took control of, the judge Gideon. With the Spirit of the Lord controlling him, Gideon was able to rally the people" (Judg. 6:34 CEV[71]). The Spirit of the Lord also came upon the judge Jephthah. We read how the Spirit took control of him as he raised up an army. ... The Spirit of God came upon King Saul to fight against the enemies of Israel. "When Saul heard their words, the Spirit of God came upon him in power, and he burned with anger" (1 Sam. 11:6 NIV[72]).[73]

When the Old Testament describes the Spirit of Jehovah dwelling within humankind, it is done prophetically, looking forward to the New Testament age. In Ezekiel 36:27, Jehovah declares, "I will put My Spirit within you and cause you to walk in My statutes, and My ordinances you shall keep and do." In another verse, Jeremiah 31:33, Jehovah declares, "I will put My law in their inward parts and write it upon their hearts; and I will be their God, and they will be My people."

---

[71] The *Contemporary English Version*. Copyright © 1995 American Bible Society. All rights reserved.

[72] *Holy Bible: New International Version*. NIV. Copyright © 1973, 1978, 1984 by International Bible Society. Used by permission of Zondervan. All rights reserved.

[73] Don Stewart, "How Did the Holy Spirit Work during the Old Testament Period?" Blue Letter Bible, accessed April 16, 2024, https://www.blueletterbible.org/faq/donstewart/donstewart437.cfm.

These verses provide a clear note of contrast to Israel's experience of failure in the Old Testament dispensation. Although God desired to make His chosen people holy, they failed again and again. Therefore, God used His prophets to speak encouraging and prophetic words to them. But these prophetic utterances were fulfilled in the New Testament dispensation.

God's heart's desire is to make His people one with Him and to gain His expression and representation within their being. In the Old Testament, no matter how much God contacted people or how much they drew near to God, God was not dwelling in them until God became flesh, the man Jesus Christ (John 1:14).

In the New Testament, God became incarnated, was crucified, and was resurrected to become a life-giving Spirit. Therefore, when the Spirit was poured out at Pentecost, the Spirit of God no longer had only divinity: He also had the humanity of Jesus. The Spirit includes Christ's incarnation, His human life, His crucifixion, His redeeming death, His resurrection, and His ascension, with the elements of Jesus's humanity. The Spirit of God includes the resurrected humanity of Jesus and the divinity of Christ.

God went through many processes to become the all-inclusive Spirit indwelling His believers. This Spirit with all the riches of God is the law of the Spirit of life working within human beings to free them from the law of sin and death. That the infinite God became a finite man is unprecedented in the history of humankind.

Through God's incarnation, God became flesh, lived a human life, was crucified, and resurrected. Through resurrection, He became the life-giving Spirit, the pneumatic Christ. Now the life-giving pneumatic Christ is able to enter into the human spirit of whomever is open and willing to receive Him. Through regeneration, the enlivened believers can worship God, praise God, live God, and express God.

1. The Spirit of God Upon God's People in the Old Testament

In the Old Testament, we see God not indwelling His people but simply being with them. In Genesis, Exodus, Psalms, and the entire Old Testament, God was with His people but not yet indwelling them. God's history in the New Testament is very different. Beginning with the Gospel of Matthew and continuing through Revelation, we see God coming into His believers and being one with them.

The New Testament reveals that God is now in His believers and is one with them. God's history in the New Testament is the history of God in His believers. Romans 8:11 says, "If the Spirit of the One who raised Jesus from the dead dwells in you, He who raised Christ from the dead will also give life to your mortal bodies through His Spirit who indwells you." Now Christ is the Spirit (2 Cor. 3:17), and He is in our spirit (2 Tim. 4:22) and is one spirit with us (1 Cor. 6:17).

This writer agrees with the Bible and scholars that there is no case of the Spirit dwelling in humans in the Old Testament. Humankind is under the slavery of sin, death, and Satan. When people believe in Christ, they are released from the old Adam and are redeemed from the authority of sin, death, and Satan.

Through Christ's death and resurrection, He became the life-giving Spirit and entered into His believers to set them free from sin, death, and Satan. If anyone is in Christ, they are saved because Christ as the Spirit has entered into their spirit. This is the blessing of the gospel.

God's way of salvation in Christ is through His blood and

the cross. God uses Christ's blood to deal with sin and the cross to deal with the sinful nature. Romans 3:23 says, "All have sinned and fall short of the glory of God." That is, everyone has sinned.

Christ shed His blood for humankind. His blood satisfied God's requirement and removed humankind's sins. Therefore, "whoever calls upon the name of the Lord shall be saved" (Rom. 10:13) without any self-effort or any payment. But the believer's personality is still the same as that of unbelievers. As believers, we are saved by the Spirit, but continually we should be washed and cleansed by the Word of God, and our being should be renewed and transformed into Christ.

The application of God's way of salvation is through the Holy Spirit. Humankind is in Adam, but God's way of salvation is in Christ. Although Christ shed His blood and dealt with humankind's sin, without the Holy Spirit, no one can see this glorious fact and no one can receive Christ through their own thought.

All that Christ accomplished for humankind is applied to believers through the work of the Holy Spirit. It is the work of the Holy Spirit that causes a human being to have faith, and this is the Christian's power. Believers are not persuaded to believe by human words. They believe because the Holy Spirit speaks through human words. No one can be saved without the work of the Holy Spirit.

Christ is the Word of God and is the manifestation of God. Before the incarnation of Christ, He was in heaven, at which time He was purely God and purely Spirit with nothing other than the element of God and Spirit in Him. In the fullness of time, God entered into the Virgin Mary to become flesh. God's becoming flesh was His putting on of human nature.

When the Lord Jesus went out to preach the gospel for

God at the age of thirty, He needed to be baptized. Then the Holy Spirit came upon Him like a dove and gave Him power to preach the gospel. He had to be anointed with the Holy Spirit outwardly in order to have the power to preach.

The principle was the same for the disciples on the day of Pentecost. Prior to that day, the disciples already had the Spirit within them as life, but they did not have the Spirit upon them as power. After they received the Spirit of life within them, the Lord told them to stay and wait in Jerusalem until the Holy Spirit was poured out on them with power. On the day of Pentecost, Peter and the other apostles preached the gospel boldly after the Holy Spirit had been poured out upon them with power.

Believers might be spiritual in their living. They may know how to discern between soul and spirit, and they may know how to walk in the spirit. However, they may be weak in evangelism, or when they have the opportunity to speak for the Lord to others, they are afraid to speak.

They may walk spiritually, but when they go to preach the gospel to people, they find they are weak, feeling that they are bound by something. They are not released and do not have the boldness or courage to speak for the Lord. This proves that although the Holy Spirit is in them as life, the Holy Spirit is not upon them as power. Therefore, they need strength—not only the infilling of the Holy Spirit, but also the outpouring of the Holy Spirit.

On the day of Pentecost, Peter and the other disciples were able to stand as witnesses of Christ because they received the Holy Spirit that day, who had descended upon them with power. Before Pentecost, Peter said many foolish things, but on the day of Pentecost, his message was clear and powerful.

In the book of Acts, there are five cases of outward receipt of the Holy Spirit. In the first case, all the disciples were empowered on the day of Pentecost, having received boldness and encouragement. They spoke boldly as the Lord led them. They also spoke in tongues, other human languages. Peter and others also had the gift of preaching.

The second case involves the Samaritan believers in Acts 8 who could see the Holy Spirit above them. There were several signs by which they could know that the Holy Spirit was upon them. When writing Acts 8, the Holy Spirit did not mention anything about speaking in tongues, but people saw the Holy Spirit come upon the saints. There was some sign by which they could know that the Holy Spirit was upon the believers.

The third case concerns Saul, who later became the apostle Paul. Immediately after Saul was saved, Ananias came to him and laid his hands on him, and Saul received the Holy Spirit. Paul later said that he spoke in tongues more than others (1 Cor. 14:18). When he received the Holy Spirit, the biblical record in Acts 9 says nothing about speaking in tongues, but he mentioned later in 1 Corinthians 14 that he spoke in tongues. Therefore, we should not claim that speaking in tongues is the first evidence that the Holy Spirit is within us. There are at least the two instances, namely, the Samaritan believers and Saul, where the Bible does not mention speaking in tongues.

The fourth case concerns the house of Cornelius. When those in his house were born again, they all received the Holy Spirit upon them and spoke in tongues (Acts 10:44–46). They received the Holy Spirit within them as life and, at the same time, received the Holy Spirit without as power. They were given life, they were given power, and they were given gifts. This is normal. In a normal state, people are saved in the same way as those of Cornelius's house. Then these people had life in their spirit, and power and gifts as their testimony.

The fifth case concerns a small group of believers in Ephesus. The apostle Paul went to them and laid his hands on them, then the Holy Spirit came upon them and they spoke in tongues (Acts 19:6), which was a manifestation of the Holy Spirit.

When the believers are filled with the Holy Spirit inwardly, they will have more of Christ in their mind, emotion, and will. When they are filled with the Holy Spirit outwardly, they will be able to preach the gospel with boldness and not be timid. In this case, two aspects of the work of the Holy Spirit can be seen in the believers. It is the same Holy Spirit, both within and without, for life and for power that God wants to give His believers.

This is the blessing of the New Testament believers. The Spirit is the blessing of God's New Testament economy. The Spirit is the processed, all-inclusive, life-giving, indwelling, consummated Spirit to be the eternal portion of all the saved ones. The Spirit is the blessing of the gospel to the Gentiles.

This was the promise to Abraham, and this promise was the glad tidings in Galatians 3:14 that, through one of Abraham's descendants, all the Gentiles would be blessed. The blessing of the promise is just the all-inclusive Spirit. The all-inclusive Spirit is the reality of Christ as the blessing to all the Gentiles. We believers should realize that the central blessing is the all-inclusive Spirit.

The all-inclusive Spirit dwells in us to grow into Christ by dispensing the divine life. The Spirit not only separates us from all old and negative things and sanctifies us unto God, but also makes us a new creation that is full of the divine essence and element, that we may grow unto maturity. The Spirit transforms us by adding more divine elements and essence into us, causing us to have a metabolic, organic change in every part of our being.

2. The Spirit In and Upon His Believers in the New Testament

In the New Testament, the Spirit is in and upon His believers. Fundamentally, the indwelling Spirit never departs from the New Testament believers (John 10:28, 14:16; Eph. 4:30). Indeed, it is clear that the Holy Spirit permanently dwells in every true believer (Rom. 8:9, 11; 1 Cor. 3:16, 12:13; Eph. 1:13).[74]

Believers should be filled with the Spirit within and without and live and walk in the Spirit and according to the Spirit (Acts 4:31b; 13:52). To be filled inwardly is to receive the fullness of the Spirit, and to be filled outwardly is to experience the outpouring of the Spirit.

There is a distinction between the New Testament and the Old Testament. During the Old Testament dispensation, the Spirit could be upon a person, such as the seventy elders of Israel (Num. 11:17, 25, 26), all Jehovah's people (v. 29), Balaam (24:2), and Othniel (Judg. 3:10), among others.

In 1 Samuel 16:13–14, the Spirit of Jehovah rushed upon David (v. 13), and the Spirit of Jehovah departed from Saul (v. 14) like clothing (Judg. 6:34). The rushing of the Spirit upon David was a confirmation of Samuel's anointing of David according to God's will and was related, not to life for salvation, but to power for outward activities (Acts 2).

The Spirit of Jehovah departing from Saul demonstrates that the Spirit in the Old Testament was not permanently with them. This is a clear warning to those who claim that the Holy Spirit indwelt the people in the Old Testament.

---

[74] "Did the Holy Spirit Come Upon or Fill the Old Testament Saints?" Never Thirsty, accessed April 16, 2024, https://www.neverthirsty.org/bible-qa/qa-archives/question/did-holy-spirit-come-upon-or-fill-old-testament-saints/.

God is still doing His work. We can see that He is proceeding according to His plan in every generation, and He is the content of human history. We need to see clearly that the work of the New Testament is primarily a work through the indwelling of the Holy Spirit within us. The Holy Spirit within us as life is the inward aspect, and the Holy Spirit upon us as power is the outward aspect.

To clearly understand the work of the Holy Spirit, we should distinguish between these two aspects. We also need to know that the Holy Spirit, who is life and who dwells within us, is the Spirit of life and the Spirit of reality, sealing us as God's heirs. Also, this Spirit dwells in us as the Comforter, the Paraclete, taking care of us in our daily life.

Although the Lord Jesus is God, He was incarnated to become a human being, the last Adam. As the last Adam, He passed through death and resurrection to become a life-giving Spirit. When we believe in Him, He enters into our spirit and imparts to us the divine life, becoming our life and life supply.

The Lord Jesus, being Lord and Christ, having the glory and the kingdom and the power, truly sits on a throne in heaven. As the Spirit of life, He dwells in our spirit. We experience the Lord Jesus as the Spirit of life dwelling within us. The glorified Christ lives in us.

Romans 8:10 says, "If Christ is in you, though the body is dead because of sin, the spirit is life because of righteousness." This verse speaks of Christ dwelling within us.

Christ is on the throne in our worship, but in our experience, Christ lives within us. Objectively, He is the enthroned Lord, but subjectively, He is the Spirit of life dwelling within us. Our union with Christ brings the guarantee of our glory in the coming Kingdom Age. Therefore, we live in the Spirit just as we live in Christ.

The gifts of the Spirit are the deposit of the Christian inheritance. Jules Gross states, "Indeed, the believer lives in the Spirit, just as he lives in Christ; in his soul the activity of the one is inseparable from that of the other. As the incorporation with Christ is a 'pledge' of the 'glory to come,' in the same way the gift of the Spirit is 'a deposit' of the inheritance for the Christian."[75]

When we live in Christ, Christ works in our spirit and spreads His life into our soul. God's goal is for us to live for Christ and for Christ to be formed in us. When we are not in the spirit, we are not able to please God.

We desire to be good by way of our natural effort, and we want to keep our own law for ourselves. Keeping the law and doing good should be done by the Holy Spirit who dwells in us. Then we will not be proud of ourselves and will not condemn others.

When we read the book of James, we see that his teaching follows the Old Testament concept rather than the New Testament concept. James speaks of the law of freedom, but in the Old Testament way of keeping the law.

According to James, believers should keep the Words of the Old Testament and be doers of the law. His concept of how to fulfill the law is obviously not according to the New Testament way. James is speaking of the teachings according to the Old Testament and encouraging believers to keep the law and be doers of the law by way of their own effort. This is not the New Testament way of living and walking according to the Spirit.

The Lord gave us free will, released us from the heavy burden of the law, and gave us the Spirit to enjoy the living Christ. When believers live according to the spirit, the Lord is

---

[75] Jules Gross, *The Divinization of the Christian according to the Greek Fathers* (Anaheim: Living Stream Ministry, 2002), 85.

there, and there is freedom. Second Corinthians 3:17 says, "The Lord is the Spirit; and where the Spirit of the Lord is, there is freedom."

When believers live by the spirit, they are released from the bondage of the law, including its ordinances, practices, and regulations. But James speaks of the law in the Old Testament way, that is, keeping the letter of the law and living the life of works.

If we become doers, then we condemn others according to their doings, and we remain in our soul to measure people according to our own law. If we walk according to the spirit, we are spontaneously freed from our own religious duty, and we experience the cross of Christ through the Spirit.

Second Corinthians 3:6 says, "The letter kills, but the Spirit gives life." The veil that lies on the hearts of the Jews when they read the law of Moses keeps them from seeing the life that is in Christ. Whenever their hearts turn to the Lord, who is the liberating Spirit, the veil is taken away.

Today our faces have been unveiled by Christ, but still we have not been freed from the law. We should dig away our condemning heart, be released from outward obligation, and be released from troublesome emotion and self-law. The Spirit, who dwells in our spirit, sets us free from every kind of bondage. When our mind is set on the spirit, our heart will be purified.

Those who keep the law according to the flesh and those who live according to the Spirit are different. After Paul preached the gospel, many Gentiles were saved. Some Jews from Judea said that Gentile believers must be circumcised and keep the law of Moses.

Later, the apostles and elders in Jerusalem decided not to require these Gentile believers to keep the law. Keeping the law of Moses by way of the flesh could not change their sinful nature.

In the Old Testament, the Israelites wanted to keep the law, but there was no supply from their spirit because their spirit was still deadened, and the Holy Spirit could not dwell in them. Therefore, there was no inward supply to energize them and empower them. In contrast, those in the New Testament economy who live according to the Spirit are delivered from their self-effort and live and cooperate with the Spirit to fulfill God's purpose.

For the Gentiles, there was no law before they were saved. And after they were saved, the Bible did not require them to keep the law. The apostles commanded them to abstain from food sacrificed to idols, from blood, from eating anything that had been strangled, and from fornication.

Acts 15:29 says, "To abstain from things that have been sacrificed to idols and blood and things strangled and fornication, from which if you carefully keep yourselves, you will do well. May you be strong."

God did not give the law to the Gentiles, both saved and unsaved. The Lord Jesus saved people so that they might have life and have it more abundantly.

Believers are no longer bound by the law; they may now grow in the life of Christ to reach maturity in their faith. When they grow in life, they live a normal Christian life in their spirit. Whenever they turn to the spirit and exercise their spirit, they can experience the cross of Christ.

According to Galatians 5:16 and 25, there are two kinds of walks in the Christian life. The first is the believer's normal daily life, mentioned in verse 16. The Greek word for walk in verse 16, *peripateo* (περιπατέω), means "to act in ordinary daily life," implying a common, habitual daily walk. The believers still have to get an education, keep a job, and take care of a home and children. This is the daily walk of believers.

Believers also need the other kind of walk, mentioned in verse 25, where a different Greek word is used for walk, *stoicheo* (στοιχέω), "walking along regulated lines with a definite goal." In order to reach the goal, believers should walk in a regulated way, march in military rank, and stay in step.

Believers should walk these two kinds of walks in their Christian life. We believers should turn to our mingled spirit. If we live according to the spirit, we are freed from sins and our sinful nature and live out Christ in our daily life. However, because we do not know or have not been trained to turn to the spirit, we still do all our doing in the natural goodness and kindness, but we sense that we are empty and poor in in experience of Christ.

Every day, in all things great and small, including speaking to others, we should not do anything by ourselves but do everything by the spirit. Therefore, Romans 8:6 says, "The mind set on the flesh is death, but the mind set on the spirit is life and peace." In this way, we can grow into Christ and be rooted and grounded in His love for God's purpose to be fulfilled.

3. Our God Being Enterable, Experienceable, and Enjoyable

When we receive Christ, we are no longer empty, for we have the reality as a real person. The reality is the person. The Gospel of John concerns not doctrine but truth, that is, reality. John 1:14 reads, "The Word became flesh and tabernacled among us (and we beheld His glory, glory as of the only begotten from the Father), full of grace and reality." John does not say that the Word who became flesh was full of theology and doctrine.

Some Christians think that truth is the same as doctrine. Such people need to see the difference between truth and doctrine. Truth is Christ as the reality. Truth is not doctrine but reality—the reality of every positive thing. Without Christ, we have no reality. Philippians 1:21 says, "To me, to live is Christ." To us, to live is not ourselves, but Christ, who is the reality.

Conversely, if we do not experience the reality, then we may elevate doctrine or theology and may follow human concepts and logic. This is evident in Gordon H. Clark's assertion that Christ's dwelling in us is by our own thinking and doctrines:

> Now, the New Testament does indeed teach a mutual indwelling of Christ and the believer. There is a very real sense in which minds interpenetrate. In 1 Corinthians 2:16 Paul asserts that "we have the mind of Christ." Christ dwells in us and we in him by our thinking and believing his doctrines. As John says in his Gospel 8:51, "He who maintains my doctrine shall not see death, ever." This is intelligible. Mysticism and pietism are not.[76]

Clark goes on to say that intimacy with God and fellowship with Him involve not mutual love or the flowing of the divine life but knowledge of theology and doctrine. It is not enough to know theology and doctrine or merely to read the Bible. If Christians have never contacted Christ by calling on Jesus's name and have not had deep fellowship in the Holy Spirit, then even though they have theology and doctrine, they still have nothing to do with Christ.

The main point that Christians should not forget is that they should subjectively experience Christ and enjoy Christ as the all-inclusive Spirit (John 3:6-8).

Clark asserted, "This intimate fellowship consists of

---

[76] Gordon H. Clark, *First John: A Commentary* (Jefferson, MD: Trinity Foundation, 1980), 120.

having the same ideas, of thinking alike, of being in extensive agreement. Hence, intimacy with God, too, consists in knowing what God thinks. That is to say, in knowing a good bit of theology."[77]

Clark's statement expresses the lack of life experience and the lack of revelation of Christ. To know God is to deeply experience Him and to touch Christ as the reality. Knowing theology well can never satisfy God and cannot satisfy human beings.

Similar to Gordon H. Clark's doctrines, Archie Hui's article "The Pneumatology of Watchman Nee" appears to be based on theological concepts of God. Hui's article refers to three Old Testament verses of the Spirit's relationship with human beings: Joseph (Gen. 41:38), Joshua (Num. 27:18), and Daniel (Dan. 5:11). He contends that these three verses prove that the Old Testament speaks of the Holy Spirit indwelling humankind. Let us look at them in more detail.

First, Genesis 41:38 speaks of Joseph: "And Pharaoh said to his servants, Can we find such a man like this, in whom the Spirit of God is?" This is what Pharaoh said to his servant. Even though the Spirit of God was with Joseph's heart, the Spirit of God did not permanently indwell Joseph's spirit. Because God had not yet dealt with humankind's original sin, people's spirit was still dead, and God could not dwell in them.

Second, Numbers 27:18 speaks of Joshua: "Jehovah said to Moses, Take Joshua the son of Nun, a man in whom is the Spirit, and lay your hand upon him." Through Moses's hand upon Joshua, the Spirit of God came upon him in power, but this was for God's move or ministry. When God anointed Joshua, He could inspire him and touch him with power. But the Spirit of God never dwelled in any human being permanently in the

---

[77] Ibid., 143.

Old Testament because the Lord Jesus had not yet dealt with the sins of humankind.

Lastly, in Daniel 5:11, the Babylonian king Belshazzar's mother said, "There is a man in your kingdom in whom is a spirit of the holy gods; and in the days of your forefather light and insight and wisdom like the wisdom of the gods were found in him [Daniel]." To know the accuracy of this verse, we can refer to Judges 15:14 and 1 Samuel 16:13; 19:20.

The principle is the same: God anointed priests, kings, and prophets with power, wisdom, and insight for His move and work on the earth. God had anointed many servants in the Old Testament to cooperate in His work. However, He could never dwell in humankind because the human spirit was deadened, and sin had not yet been erased until Christ died and was resurrected.

In the Old Testament, the Spirit of God had not yet passed through the processes of death and resurrection and was only divine, but the Holy Spirit in the New Testament is the One who is both divine and human. Christ is God entering into us, and Christ is also His believers entering into God.

Incarnation is God entering into humankind, and death and resurrection are we, the believers, entering into God. "God's entering into man began with the incarnation of the Lord Jesus. Hence, in the Old Testament there was no such thing as God entering into man because at that time incarnation had not yet begun, and God and man had not yet been mingled together."[78]

Christ, who passed through incarnation, human living, crucifixion, and resurrection, became the pneumatic Christ, the life-giving Spirit. He is both divine and human, possessing both natures. The only begotten Son of God (John 3:16) became the firstborn Son of God (Rom. 8:29) in His resurrection.

---

[78] Witness Lee, *Spiritual Reality* (Anaheim: Living Stream Ministry, 2002), 115.

The outpouring of the Spirit after Christ's ascension was to carry out His heavenly ministry on earth and build up His Body, the church (Matt. 16:18). When believers call on the Lord and exercise their spirit, the divine elements are wrought into their inner being, and they experience more of Christ.

Now the Lord is the Spirit. He dwells in believers who have been washed by the precious blood of Jesus. First Corinthians 6:19–20 says, "Do you not know that your body is a temple of the Holy Spirit within you, whom you have from God, and you are not your own? For you have been bought with a price. So then glorify God in your body."

The Old Testament Israelites had not yet been washed by the blood of Jesus Christ; therefore, the Spirit could not indwell them, but the power of the Spirit came upon prophets, kings, and priests powerfully so that they were able to cooperate in the work of God.

The New Testament believers have been sanctified through Christ's blood in the Holy Spirit and by the Father's Word. The all-inclusive Christ as the life-giving Spirit is fulfilling His New Testament economy by working within them and upon them.

C. The Difference Between John the Baptist's and Jesus's Ministries

Third, an assertion has been made that there was no difference in the work of the Holy Spirit in John the Baptist and in the Lord Jesus. The people on the other side of this argument declare that the Lord Jesus's ministry was quite different from John the Baptist's. One scholar, James D. G. Dunn, highlighted that John's water baptism was only a shadow and symbol of Christ's Spirit baptism.

In the Old Testament dispensation of law, John was the

last and greatest of the prophets (Matt. 11:13; Luke 7:28). In contrast, the Lord Jesus was the first man in the New Testament dispensation of grace and reality. John prepared the way directly for the incarnated God, and John's being was filled with the Holy Spirit from his mother's womb. This indicates that the New Testament is the new dispensational age. The name of the Holy Spirit is also new. Nevertheless, Jesus and John the Baptist were still in the Old Testament age. "In the Old Testament, we do not find the Holy Spirit dwelling within man.

The difference between the Old Testament and the New Testament is the Holy Spirit dwelling within man."[79] Elizabeth and Zechariah were filled with the Holy Spirit for their prophetic utterances, but they were not indwelt by the Holy Spirit; they were empowered by the Spirit to carry out His purpose (Luke 1:41, 67).

1. The Transitory Period Between the Old and New Dispensations

The birth of John the Baptist was transitional between the Old Testament dispensation and the New Testament dispensation. John preached a baptism of repentance and prepared people's hearts to receive Christ.

James D. G. Dunn mentioned: "John's water baptism is only a shadow and symbol of the Christ's Spirit baptism. The contrast between the two baptisms is the contrast between John and Jesus—the antithesis of preparation and fulfillment, of shadow and substance."[80]

The Lord Jesus's birth is quite different from that of John the Baptist. The New Testament begins with a great contrast between

---

[79] Watchman Nee, *CWWN*, vol. 41, 157.
[80] James D. G. Dunn, *Baptism in the Holy Spirit* (London: SCM, 1970), 19.

these two births. The conception of John was strikingly different in essence from that of Jesus the Savior. The conception of the Savior was God's incarnation (John 1:14), constituted not only of the divine power but also of the divine life added to Jesus's life. "From His birth, the Lord was not just a man filled outwardly with the Holy Spirit as John was, but a God-man constituted of the divine essence from the Holy Spirit and the human essence from Mary.

When the Lord was baptized by John in the Jordan, however, the Spirit descended upon Him in power for His ministry, His work."[81] This proves that Jesus experienced another aspect of the work of the Holy Spirit at this time. It was the Holy Spirit descending upon Him with divine power that enabled Him to work for God. When He was conceived, He was conceived in Mary of the Holy Spirit as life (Matt. 1:18, 20), and later, at His baptism, He experienced the Holy Spirit as power (Matt. 3:16).

Christ was filled with the Holy Spirit inwardly and outwardly. Essentially, Christ's divinity is God, but economically Christ in His humanity needed to be baptized to carry out God's plan. For this reason, the Spirit as a dove came upon Him.

According to Hui's article, "While Mark 1:10 describes the Spirit coming down and entering 'into him' (eis auton), both Matthew 3:16 and Luke 3:22 speak of the Spirit coming 'upon him' (ep' auton)."[82] However, the most commonly used Bible translations say that the Spirit as a dove descended upon Jesus.

According to *The New Greek/English Interlinear New Testament*, Mark 1:10 is translated as follows: "καὶ εὐθὺς ἀναβαίνων ἐκ τοῦ ὕδατος εἶδεν σχιζομένους τοὺς οὐρανοὺς καὶ τὸ πνεῦμα ὡς περιστερὰν καταβαῖνον εἰζ αὐτόν."[83] In English,

---

[81] Jim Batten, "The Corporate God," *Affirmation & Critique* 10, no 2 (October 2005): 105.

[82] Archie Hui, "*The Pneumatology of Watchman Nee*," 10.

[83] Robert K. Brown and Philip W. Comfort, s.v. Mark 1:10, *The New Greek/English Interlinear New Testament* (Carol Stream, IL: Tyndale House, 1990).

this verse is, "And just as He was coming up out of the water, He saw the heavens torn apart and the Spirit descending like a dove on Him."[84]

The Recovery Version of the Bible reads, "And immediately, coming up out of the water, He saw the heavens being parted and the Spirit as a dove descending upon Him."[85] Before the Spirit of God descended and came upon Him, the Lord Jesus was born of the Holy Spirit (Luke 1:35). He was essentially filled with the Holy Spirit.

For Christ's earthly ministry, He was baptized by John the Baptist economically, but intrinsically He is God Himself, and He was filled with the Spirit essentially.

Some scholars insist that John the Baptist's baptism and the Lord Jesus Christ's baptism were the same, but this is only an outward view. John the Baptist had said that he baptized people in water unto repentance but that there was another One who would baptize people in the Holy Spirit unto life. The baptism of the Lord Jesus means to be born again with water and the Spirit (John 3:5).

The *New International Version* presents the verse this way: "As Jesus was coming up out of the water, he saw heaven being torn open and the Spirit descending on him like a dove."[86] The King James Version also translated this verse using *upon*. When Jesus was baptized, the Spirit of God was already within Him. Luke 2:40 says, "The little child grew and became strong, being filled with wisdom." The footnote reads, "Grew in stature (v. 52) and became strong in spirit."[87]

As can be seen in the work of the Holy Spirit in John the

---

[84] Ibid.

[85] Witness Lee, *Holy Bible Recovery Version*, Mark 1:10.

[86] International Bible Society, the *New International Version* (Colorado Springs: Biblica, 1978), Mark 1:10.

[87] Witness Lee, *Holy Bible Recovery Version*, Luke 2:40, footnote 1.

Baptist and the Lord Jesus, the two ministries are not the same. And through Jesus's baptism, we can see that the Holy Spirit came upon Him for His ministry. According to what we have discussed so far, Mark 1:10, Matthew 3:16, and Luke 3:22 are all absolutely right that the Holy Spirit descended *upon* Jesus.

In the New Testament, the Holy Spirit's work has two aspects: the inward aspect for life and living, and the outward aspect for power and moving. The Spirit's descending upon Jesus as a dove signifies that God empowered Him with the Spirit for His ministry to God. The Lord Jesus was baptized by John the Baptist and led up into the wilderness by the Spirit.

Matthew 4:1 says, "Jesus was led up into the wilderness by the Spirit to be tempted by the devil." The newly anointed Jesus was led by the Spirit to fast for this period of time that He might enter into His earthly ministry. While fasting, He was tempted by the devil and defeated him with the Word of God.

Luke 4:18–19 says, "The Spirit of the Lord is upon Me, because He has anointed Me to announce the gospel to the poor; He has sent Me to proclaim release to the captives, and recovery of sight to the blind, to send away in release those who are oppressed, to proclaim the acceptable year of the Lord, the year of jubilee." God has poured out His Spirit upon the Lord Jesus for His ministry.

John the Baptist, who baptized the Lord Jesus, was filled with the Holy Spirit, but he did not have the indwelling Spirit because the time had not yet come for the indwelling Spirit. According to Matthew 11:2–3, "Now when John heard in the prison of the works of the Christ, he sent word through his disciples, and said to Him, Are You the Coming One, or should we expect another?"

John the Baptist knew that Christ was the coming One, and he strongly recommended Him to the people (John 1:26–36).

After that, he was put into prison, and there he waited, expecting that Christ would do something to deliver him. The Lord Jesus did many things for others, but He did not do anything for John the Baptist. This was the reason John tried to provoke the Lord Jesus to do something for him.

In John 7:22–23 we have the Lord's answer to John the Baptist's question: "Go and report to John what you have seen and heard: the blind are receiving sight, the lame are walking, the lepers are being cleansed, and the deaf are hearing, the dead are being raised, and the good news is being brought to the poor; and blessed is he who is not stumbled in Me."

The Lord first spoke of the blind receiving sight. There was no such miracle in the Old Testament. By this, He gave clear evidence to John that only the Messiah could perform such a miracle (Isa. 35:5). John knew that although the Lord could have done something, it was right for Him not to do anything. John likely gained strength from the words of the Lord and thereby was enabled to be martyred.

2. John the Baptist Being Filled with the Economical Spirit

John the Baptist was the inaugurator who brought in the New Testament age. John the Baptist's background included knowledge of many ordinances for living and many religious regulations related to service to God, including the priestly service. He was an Israelite born into the tribe of serving priests, that is, the tribe of Levi.

As one who was born a priest, and according to the regulations of the Old Testament, John should have spent much time in the temple. However, he did not stay in the temple; he lived in the wilderness. He put aside human religion, human culture, all of humankind's traditions, and the tradition of serving God, abandoning them all. This strongly indicates that God's heart's desire is contrary to religion and culture. The old way of worshipping God according to the Old Testament was fulfilled, and a new way was brought in.

"The word of God came to John, the son of Zachariah, in the wilderness. And he came into all the region surrounding the Jordan, proclaiming a baptism of repentance for forgiveness of sins" (Luke 3:2–3).

To baptize people is to bury them by immersing them in the water, which signifies death, the act indicating that the repentant people are buried and become nothing. It also signifies the end of the old person and the beginning of the new life. Therefore, John's baptism not only terminated those who repented, but also brought them to Christ for life.

Baptism in the Bible means death and resurrection. To be baptized with water is to be cast into death and buried. To be raised from the water means to be resurrected from the dead.

Although John preached the baptism of repentance, the goal of his ministry was Jesus Christ, the Son of God. He realized that he was just a messenger (Mal. 3:1) sent by Jehovah of hosts to lead people to Jesus Christ, the Son of God, and to exalt Him as the goal of his ministry. John testified that he baptized with water but that the coming Christ would baptize with the Holy Spirit and fire.

John the Baptist had the spirit and power of Elijah and did the work of Elijah in turning many Israelites to the Lord their God (Luke 1:16–17). Furthermore, he was the first person in the New Testament to be filled with the Holy Spirit. Therefore, in type, he was the coming Elijah. In Matthew 11:14, the Lord Jesus spoke to the disciples concerning John the Baptist: "If you are willing to receive it, he is Elijah, who is to come."

John the Baptist was filled with the Holy Spirit even from his mother's womb. He was filled with the Spirit outwardly as power for God's ministry. He could minister in such a way to separate people for God and bring them back to God. He was the forerunner of the Lord Jesus and the voice of the one crying in the wilderness (John 1:23).

John the Baptist referred to the Lord as "He who baptizes in the Holy Spirit" (1:33). He acknowledged, "I did not know Him, but He who sent me to baptize in water, He said to me, He upon whom you see the Spirit descending and abiding upon Him, this is He who baptizes in the Holy Spirit" (1:33). When John baptized the Lord Jesus in water, he saw the Spirit descending upon Him as a dove out of heaven (John 1:32; Matt. 3:13–17).

In Matthew 17:12, the Lord continued, saying, "But I say to you that Elijah already came, and they did not recognize him, but did to him whatever they wished." This refers to John the Baptist (Matt. 17:13), who came in the spirit and power of Elijah (Luke 1:13–17) and was rejected (Matt. 11:18) and beheaded in prison (14:3–12).

John had been sent by God as a messenger before Christ to prepare the way for Christ so that the people might be turned to God and receive the heavenly King and the heavenly kingdom. In short, the purpose of John the Baptist's ministry was to pave the way for the New Testament age.

When Christ came to work, John the Baptist needed to stop his work and withdraw from his position, leaving only Christ in the field. And all those who had followed John needed to go to Christ. John was the forerunner of Christ, a voice crying out to pave the way for Christ and introduce Him.

John the Baptist preached a baptism of repentance and prepared people's hearts to receive Christ. He had the spirit and power of Elijah to change people's hearts and turn them to Christ. He testified of Christ and actively proclaimed to his disciples that Christ was the bridegroom who was coming to marry the church, that John himself was only a friend of the Bridegroom, and that this Christ must increase and John must decrease.

John 3:30 says, "He must increase, but I must decrease." John told his disciples that Jesus is the Christ. Not only were other people going to Jesus, but also John's disciples needed to go to Him. The bride is the increase of the Bridegroom. In order for Christ to increase, our old "I" should decrease, which is the way for Him to have the church. The church is the bride of Christ.

Matthew 11:11-13 says, "Truly I say to you, among those born of women there has not arisen one greater than John the Baptist, yet he who is least in the kingdom of the heavens is greater than he. But from the days of John the Baptist until now, the kingdom of the heavens is taken by violence, and violent men seize it. For all the prophets and the law prophesied until John."

In Matthew 11:11 the Lord said that although John was greater than all the prophets, he was the least in the kingdom of the heavens. "John did not prophesy. Instead, he pointed out the Lord to people, "Behold, the Lamb of God!" (John 1:29). This is where his greatness lies. He was great with respect to the time that he was in; his opportunity was different from that of others."[88]

John the Baptist was in a transitory period, greater than those who preceded him, but smaller than those who were to come after him. Compared to the Old Testament prophets, John was greater, but compared to the people of the New Testament, John was smaller. All the prophets before John prophesied that

[88] Watchman Nee, *CWWN*, vol. 15, 101.

Christ would come, but John testified that Christ had come. The prophets were looking forward to Christ, but John saw Christ. Therefore, John was greater than all the prophets.

Although John saw the incarnated Christ and introduced Him to people, John did not have the resurrected Christ indwelling him. We, the New Testament people, have the indwelling Christ in our spirit.

John could say, "Here is Christ," but the kingdom people can say, "To me to live is Christ" (Phil. 1:21). Therefore, the least in the kingdom of the heavens is greater than John the Baptist. Whether believers are greater or lesser depends upon their relationship with Christ. Christ is the decisive factor. The closer they are to Christ, the greater they are.

John the Baptist was close to Christ, but he was not as close to Him as the believers because believers have Christ within their spirit. To put it another way: Christ is in the believers, and they are in Christ. Their relationship with Christ is most intimate because Christ is united with them. And they are united with Him, even joined to Him. First Corinthians 6:17 says, "He who is joined to the Lord is one spirit." This intimate relationship with Christ makes believers of Christ greater than the Old Testament believers.

John the Baptist was filled with the Holy Spirit even from his mother's womb, but he did not have the Spirit indwelling him. But New Testament believers are those who are united with the Spirit of Christ. God is in Christ, and Christ became the Spirit (1 Cor. 15:45). The Spirit indwelling believers is Christ, and God is indwelling them, causing them to be joined to Christ. Therefore, one who is saved and belongs to Christ and God does indeed have the indwelling Holy Spirit.

3. Jesus Christ Being Filled with the Essential and Economical Spirit

The Holy Spirit in power descended upon Jesus at His baptism. He already had the Holy Spirit in essence from His conception, meaning He had the Holy Spirit essentially within, and He received the outpouring of the Spirit economically. The importance of baptism is that although He was the Son of God who came to be the Savior of humankind, He needed to be baptized because everything natural must be terminated in *God's economy*.[89]

The Lord was baptized to allow Himself to be put into death and resurrection so that He might minister, not in the natural way, but in the way of resurrection. In God's New Testament dispensation, Christ has ended the Old Testament dispensation and taken it away (Rom. 10:4; Heb. 10:9) and has brought in the New Testament dispensation.

With the Lord Jesus, believers see two aspects of the Holy Spirit. First, the Lord was conceived of the Holy Spirit (Luke 1:35; Matt. 1:18, 20). Then at the age of thirty, when He came forth to minister, the Holy Spirit descended upon Him, and He was baptized in the Holy Spirit (Luke 3:21–22).

The Lord's being conceived of the Spirit was a matter of the Spirit of life essentially, but His being baptized in the Holy Spirit was a matter of the Spirit descending upon Him economically for God's work. Hence, the gift of the Holy Spirit for the Lord's conception was essential, whereas the gift of the Holy Spirit for His ministry was economical.

Since the Lord Jesus was essentially conceived of the Holy

---

[89] God's economy is God's plan, His arrangement, and His method of household administration for dispensing Himself into His chosen people so that He may accomplish His purposes.

Spirit, the Spirit became the essence of His being, meaning the Lord had the divine essence of the conceiving Spirit. He also received the human essence from the Virgin Mary. Because He was conceived with the divine essence and born with the human essence, He was born as a God-man. Therefore, He was both God and man, fully God and completely man.

For thirty years the Lord Jesus lived on earth as a God-man. At the age of thirty, He began His ministry, for which He needed the Spirit of God to descend upon Him economically, not essentially. Put another way, the coming of the Spirit upon the Lord Jesus was for God's economy. For His existence, He essentially needed His divine essence, the Holy Spirit, but in order to carry out God's economy, He needed the Holy Spirit to descend upon Him economically. When the man Jesus lived on earth for thirty-three and a half years, God lived in Him.

When Jesus was on the earth, the fullness of the Godhead dwelled in Him. Christ was the eternal Word even before He was incarnated. From the time Christ Jesus became flesh and put on a human body, the fullness of the Godhead began to dwell in Him in a bodily way (Phil. 3:21), and it abides in Him now and forever. That the fullness of the Godhead dwells bodily in Christ means that the Godhead dwells in Him in a real and practical way. Now that the fullness of the Godhead dwells bodily in Christ as the divine person, it is visible, tangible, and receivable.

Colossians 2:9 says that the fullness of the Godhead dwells in Jesus bodily. This means that the riches of the Godhead are fully expressed in Him. When this man Jesus lived on earth, He lived in such a way that everyone around Him saw the fullness of the Godhead, which flowed from Him. The fullness of the Godhead not only dwelled in Him but also flowed out of Him. When He lived in the carpenter's house in Nazareth,

He was the embodiment of the fullness of the Godhead. As the embodiment of the fullness of the Godhead, He possessed all that the Father had.

In John 16:15, Jesus said that everything the heavenly Father has is His. Because He lived as the embodiment of the Father, the Son, and the Holy Spirit, He inherited everything that God the Father had. Even at the age of twelve, He lived in such a way that everyone saw the fullness of the Godhead flowing from Him. It was not just His work or office; it was His life. He lived the fullness of the Godhead. Therefore, He could say, "He who has seen Me has seen the Father" (14:9). Christ is God—the manifestation of God Himself.

Colossians 2:9 says, "In Him dwells all the fullness of the Godhead bodily." The fullness of the Godhead dwells as a divine person in Christ bodily, it is visible, touchable, and experienceable. "The fullness of the Godhead dwells as a person in the incarnated Christ bodily, that is, in Christ with a human body. Hence, the word bodily in verse 9 points to the physical body that Christ put on in His humanity, indicating that all the fullness of the Godhead dwells in Christ as One who has a human body."[90]

The verb to dwell indicates that the fullness of the Godhead is a person. The fullness of the Godhead is personified. Before Christ's incarnation, the fullness of the Godhead dwelled in Him as the eternal Word. The fullness of the Godhead is threefold: the Father, the Son, and the Holy Spirit. All the fullness of the Godhead now enters into His believers by the Holy Spirit, becoming their person and working in them.

Now, in John 20:22, the disciples received the Holy Spirit

---

[90] Witness Lee, *Experiencing, Enjoying, and Expressing Christ in the Epistles (61)*, vol. 2 of *The Conclusion of the New Testament: Experiencing, Enjoying, and Expressing Christ* (Anaheim: Living Stream Ministry, 1996), 3569.

essentially for their spiritual life and their spiritual living. After receiving the Holy Spirit for their spiritual life, they still needed to receive the Spirit economically so that they could carry out God's work as the continuation of the Lord's ministry. Since the Lord carried out God's economy with an economical Spirit, the disciples had to carry out God's economy with the same Spirit. Therefore, after receiving the Spirit essentially, the disciples had to receive the Spirit economically on the day of Pentecost in Acts 2.

In John 20:22, it was emphasized that the disciples received the Holy Spirit essentially for their spiritual life and existence. Before John 20, that is, before the Lord's death and resurrection, the disciples were not spiritual; they lived according to the fallen natural carnal life.

Even after the Lord revealed His death and resurrection to them the third time (Mark 10:32–34), the disciples were still debating who was the greatest (Mark 10:35–45). Furthermore, Peter was obviously in his natural being when he denied the Lord. But after Christ's death and resurrection, the disciples received the essential Spirit as the source of their spiritual existence.

As previously mentioned, the Lord Jesus and John the Baptist were fundamentally different. During the age of the Old Testament and the law, John was the last and greatest prophet (Matt. 11:13; Luke 7:28). In contrast, the Lord Jesus was the first person in the New Testament dispensation of grace and reality.

In God's New Testament economy, Christ ended the Old Testament age and brought in the New Testament age. Even though John the Baptist was filled with the Holy Spirit economically for God's work, he was just a dispensational instrument used by God. He simply prepared the way through baptism for Christ's ministry on the earth.

Unlike John the Baptist, the Lord Jesus had both the essential and economical Spirit. First, the Holy Spirit came as the divine essence for the conception and birth of the Lord Jesus (Luke 1:35; Matt. 1:18, 20). Second, the Spirit also came to Jesus Christ as the divine power for the anointing of Christ (Matt. 3:16). He was already born of the Holy Spirit and had the Holy Spirit in Him essentially, but He needed the Holy Spirit as the divine power economically. God came to anoint Him with the Holy Spirit as the economical Spirit to carry out His earthly ministry.

There is no forgiveness of sins without the redemptive death and resurrection of Christ. Without judicial redemption, God could not come into humankind, and humankind would never be released from the bondage of the slavery of sin and condemnation of the law.

Christ's redeeming death was determined by God in eternity and was foretold by the prophets in Old Testament times. This proves that the death of Christ was planned by God according to His good pleasure and announced in advance through the prophets (Eph. 1:7–10).

Now Christ has accomplished everything, having attained and obtained all things in His ascension. All authority in heaven and on earth has been given to Him, all the enemies have been subjected under His feet, and He is now head over all things (Matt. 28:18; Eph. 1:22b). He is now in the heavens, but He is also in the spirit of believers as the pneumatic Christ.

John 6:63 says, "It is the Spirit who gives life; the flesh profits nothing; the words which I have spoken to you are Spirit and are life." The Spirit is living and real. When people receive His Words by exercising their spirit, they get the Spirit, who is life. Unlike the ministry of Moses in the Old Testament, the ministry of the apostles in the New Testament is not of the dead letter of the law, but of a living Spirit who gives life.

Second Corinthians 3:6 says, "The letter kills, but the Spirit gives life." When we say that the letter kills, it means that mere doctrine, the knowledge of the letter, causes people to pay attention to things other than life. The letter has no supply of life and no anointing; that which is of Christ has life.

We should have another life, a higher life, even the highest life. In the universe, no life is higher than God's life. The Lord is the Spirit (2 Cor. 3:17). The Spirit gives life (John 6:63) and is the living and flowing Spirit. When we contact the Spirit, we become alive and vital.

D. Distinguishing the Day of Resurrection from the Day of Pentecost

Fourth, a certain group contends that John 20:22 is merely symbolic and that John wrote for his own literary and theological purposes. And they say that what the early disciples experienced at Easter should not be viewed as a pattern for post-Pentecostal believers today.[91]

The people on the other side of this argument assert that after Jesus's resurrection, He breathed His life into His disciples in John 20:22, which is now continually experienced wherever the gospel is preached. And on the day of Pentecost, His disciples received the power of the Holy Spirit in Acts 2, which is continuing until now.

On the day of resurrection, the Lord Jesus breathed into the disciples and told them to receive the Holy Spirit. After the disciples received the Holy Spirit, He never left them but dwelled in them permanently. This was the beginning of Christ's heavenly ministry.

---

[91] Archie Hui, "*The Pneumatology of Watchman Nee*," 19–20.

Before His ascension, the Lord Jesus charged His disciples to wait for the Holy Spirit, and after ten days the disciples received the power of the Holy Spirit for His ministry on the day of Pentecost.

This prophecy in Acts 1:4–5, "He [Jesus] met together with them, He charged them not to depart from Jerusalem, but to wait for the promise of the Father, which, He said, you heard from Me; for John baptized with water, but you shall be baptized in the Holy Spirit not many days from now" was fulfilled on the day of Pentecost.

1. The Difference Between the Gentle Breathing and the Mighty Wind

John 20:22 and Acts chapter 2 are different. It is the difference between the gentle breathing and the mighty wind. In John 20:22, the Lord Jesus gently breathed the Holy Spirit into His disciples with tender care. In Acts 2, the outpouring of the Holy Spirit was the blowing of a strong, mighty wind (v. 2).

This outward experience is different from the inward filling of the Holy Spirit. The inward filling of the Holy Spirit is for inner life, and the outpouring of the Holy Spirit is for outward service and work. The disciples were outwardly filled with the Holy Spirit (Acts 2:4), which shows that the outward filling of the Holy Spirit is the baptism of the Holy Spirit.

God sent John the Baptist to baptize people in water before the reality of the baptism of the Holy Spirit. When John baptized people in water, he said that the Lord Jesus would baptize people in the Holy Spirit, meaning that they would receive their baptism in the Holy Spirit. The Lord Jesus baptized them in the Holy Spirit as the power on the day of Pentecost.

Concerning "Receive the Holy Spirit" in John 20:22, the

Johannine Pentecost school regards this verse as being merely symbolic and contends that John wrote it for his own literary and theological purposes. "The theme is that of Luke's story of Pentecost, and, if Pentecost has not precisely replaced Easter in John's interest, it has certainly become coincidental with Easter."[92] Archie Hui agreed with G. W. H. Lampe's statement of unbelief.

These writers may have knowledge of the biblical story and study of theology, but they surely have not touched the indwelling Holy Spirit and have not been led by the Holy Spirit. God's Word is not limited to doctrine, knowledge, or the dead letter of the law.

God came to be the believers' enjoyment; this is unfathomable grace. Only God is true. He is real, and He is experiential. Without God, the whole world would be only a source of vanity and misery. The disciples' experience on the day of resurrection and the day of Pentecost is reality and fact. Under the shining light of God, humankind's real condition is revealed. Satan is causing people to forget their origin.

From the beginning, God's intention was that the human race would live not by their own life but by God's life. For this reason, after God created Adam, God placed him in front of the tree of life.

Before Adam's fall, God wanted him to eat of the tree of life and to live by the tree of life as the Word of God. Whereas in God's creation human nature was good, after the fall, human nature became sinful. We were created by God, we became fallen, and we were redeemed and regenerated through Jesus Christ.

Regeneration means that people should not live by their natural human life but by God's life as the Word of God. We

---

[92] G. W. H. Lampe, *God as Spirit* (Oxford, UK: Oxford University Press, 1977), 9.

believers now have two lives in us: the created life as the natural life and the regenerated life as the divine life.

Our natural self has been terminated by Christ on the cross. We have been not only terminated but also regenerated. We were terminated by Christ's death, and we were germinated by Christ's resurrection.

2. The Pneumatic Christ Breathing into His Disciples for Their Life

Resurrection is the Holy Spirit, and the Holy Spirit is the reality of resurrection. After the Lord's resurrection and ascension, the Holy Spirit was poured out. Now the Holy Spirit is the Spirit of resurrection. Resurrection comes before ascension, and ascension comes after resurrection.

W. H. Griffith Thomas affirmed that in the Bible, there is a reason for each portion: John 20:22 is the power of Christ's resurrection, and Acts 2:1–4 is the power of His ascension. Thomas further corroborated this by citing other authors:

> The question has often been asked in what relation the gift of Easter Day stands to the gift of Whitsunday [Pentecost]. Bishop Westcott, following Godet, replies that "the one answers to the power of resurrection and the other to the power of the ascension," i.e., the one brought the grace of quickening, the other that of endowment. We cannot fail to recall the divine "breathing" of Genesis 2:7, expressive of life. But besides this, if we may judge from the words that follow, the Easter gift was specially connected with the future work of the Body of Christ.[93]

---

[93] W. H. Griffith Thomas, *The Holy Spirit of God* (London: Longmans, Green & Co., 1913), 62–63, quoted in Swete, *The Holy Spirit in the New*

W. H. Griffith Thomas said that Christ's Easter gifts are specifically related to "the future work of the Body of Christ."[94] While Christ was in the body, He said He would die and be resurrected to come again in another form. Because of Christ's resurrection, He fulfilled His words in John 7:38–39: "He who believes into Me, as the Scripture said, out of his innermost being shall flow rivers of living water. But this He said concerning the Spirit, whom those who believed into Him were about to receive; for the Spirit was not yet, because Jesus had not yet been glorified."

Resurrection means overcoming because Christ overcame death through resurrection, and ascension means transcendence because Christ transcended everything in His ascension. The fulfillment of this Word occurred when the resurrected and glorified Christ appeared to the disciples and said to them to receive the Holy Spirit, then He entered into them.

Andrew Murray contended for the personhood of the Spirit:

> God be praised! Jesus has been glorified: there is now the Spirit of the glorified Jesus; we have received Him. In the Old Testament only the unity of God was revealed; when the Spirit was mentioned, it was always as His Spirit, the power by which God was working: He was not known on earth as a Person. In the New Testament the Trinity is revealed; with Pentecost the Holy Spirit descended as a Person to dwell in us.[95]

Testament (Eugene: Wipf and Stock, 1998), 167. See also W. T. P. Wolston, *Another Comforter* (Addison, IL: Bible Truth, 1982), 131–34.

[94] W. H. Griffith Thomas, *The Holy Spirit of God*, 63.

[95] Andrew Murray, *The Spirit of the Glorified Jesus* (Anaheim: Living Stream Ministry, 1994), 7–8.

Jesus became the life-giving Spirit and came into the believers as the pneumatic Christ. Believers are witnesses who testify that Christ is glorified. In the book of Acts, the apostles, the church, and the believers were the testimony of the resurrected and ascended Christ before other people. Sin, the world, and death had not overcome them because they were in Christ's death, resurrection, and ascension.

The Holy Spirit can be obtained and experienced by those who have passed through the cross. Christ is the life, and the cross is the way. Without the cross, believers cannot experience the life of Christ. Only those who have passed through the cross can overcome hardships and do the work of the Lord on this earth. Although He is invisible to human eyes, He is carrying out His heavenly ministry.

In the eyes of humankind, the earthly history of the Lord ended with His resurrection and ascension. In fact, there is only the prototype in the Gospels, but there are many copies in Acts. There is one grain of wheat in the Gospels but many grains in Acts. Just as Jesus of Nazareth followed God rather than people, His disciples, Peter and John, followed God rather than people.

Jesus of Nazareth did not focus on His own interests, nor did Peter and John on theirs. As a grain of wheat, Christ as the divine seed has produced many grains of wheat by their experience of His life-releasing death for the multiplication of the divine life. This reproduction is possible through the indwelling Holy Spirit because He lives and unites with believers, giving them strength and encouragement.

The apostles were the expansion and spreading of Christ, the living testimony of Christ's resurrection and ascension. Because their works and actions were from the Holy Spirit, the work done by the Holy Spirit was in resurrection and ascension.

The Spirit is the transfiguration of Christ. Therefore, what proceeds from the Spirit is from Christ. The actions and works of the apostles were entirely motivated by the Holy Spirit. In other words, Christ was motivating them in their spirit. This is what it is to be led by the Spirit, not by natural human effort or zeal, to become the testimony and enlargement of Christ.

When Christ lived on earth, He never did anything by Himself or spoke anything of Himself or from Himself. Whatever He did and spoke was by the Father (John 5:19, 30; 7:16; 8:28; 12:49–50). For thirty-three and a half years He lived a crucified life, always living by the Father. To live in resurrection means that we reject our natural life and are conformed to the death of Christ. To do this requires growth in life.

To grow into Christ in all things means to grow into Him in every aspect of the believer's daily life. If Christ governs the believer's mind, emotion, will, and conscience, and is allowed to take root in their inward parts, they will grow into Christ as the head in every way. He is constantly working within believers.

As believers cooperate with Him, they are renewed little by little each day and grow into Christ. This is to be in the flow of the Holy Spirit. Saints are built up as the Body of Christ under the direction of the indwelling Spirit, and Christ makes His home in their heart (Eph. 3:17).

Christians' growth in life is the growth into Christ the head, and their function in *the Body of Christ*[96] is a function stemming out from the head. When believers are in the Holy Spirit, they will be led by the Holy Spirit just as the apostles were and will be a testimony of Christ.

---

[96] To say that the church is the Body of Christ means that the church is a part of Christ. The church is Christ because the church and Christ have one life; thus, the content of the church is Christ. First Corinthians 12:12 says, "Even as the body is one and has many members, yet all the members of the body, being many, are one body, so also is the Christ." The church is joined to Christ and has His life and nature.

The apostles were in the stream of the Holy Spirit. Their works were inside the body. The work in Acts was all of one flow because everything was of the church as *the corporate body*,[97] and those who were serving worked in one body and in one spirit. This stream started in Jerusalem and went to Samaria, where the church, the Body of Christ, was further developed. Later, this stream went to Antioch and then to Asia Minor.

The work of the apostles was to lead people to receive the Holy Spirit. The apostles helped people to experience the Holy Spirit both inwardly and outwardly. They and their work depended on the Holy Spirit.

Believers were witnesses of Christ's resurrection and ascension because they received Christ through the Holy Spirit and realized that they had been freed from the power of sin and death. Therefore, they were witnesses of Christ and channels of life.

Our God today as the reality of resurrection is Christ as the life-giving Spirit. Our God, unlike the Jewish God, is not only divine but also human. He is not only God but also human, with Christ's death and its effectiveness and with His resurrection with its power, all compounded together to be the life-giving Spirit, the ultimate consummation of the processed Triune God. The Triune God was embodied in Christ, who eventually became the life-giving Spirit, the pneumatic Christ, who is the reality of resurrection.

Today we have the consummated Triune God, the pneumatic

---

[97] The corporate body is Christ and the church. In Christ's resurrection, He raised up all His believers together with Him and enlarged His body into the corporate body, which is the church, as the corporate dwelling place of God. The corporate body built by Christ in resurrection is altogether a new creation, not according to the old nature of the flesh, but according to the new nature of God's life.

Christ, and the all-inclusive life-giving Spirit as the reality of resurrection. Resurrection is a living person, the Lord Jesus Christ (John 11:25). He is the resurrection, and in resurrection He has become the life-giving Spirit. For us today, the reality of resurrection is Christ as the life-giving Spirit.

3. The Outpouring of the Spirit for His Testimony and Increase

The Holy Spirit is not only within believers but also outside them. The outward filling of the Holy Spirit is signified by the water of baptism that covers believers when they are immersed. On the day of Pentecost, the powerful Holy Spirit, like a violent rushing wind, filled the upper room.

The disciples sitting therein were spiritually baptized with the power of the Holy Spirit. Through this event, we see that the outward filling of the Holy Spirit is like baptism. When believers speak of being baptized with the Holy Spirit, it means that they have put on the Holy Spirit and are covered with the Holy Spirit.

John 20:22 and Acts 2:4 can be distinguished. The disciples were filled inwardly and essentially with the Spirit in them, and were filled outwardly and economically with the Spirit upon them. Every believer in Christ should experience both aspects of the Holy Spirit.

When converts receive the Lord Jesus, at that time, the Lord enters into their spirit. Some people receive dynamic salvation, but even so, most converts do not know about the Spirit. Some converts doubt their salvation even after receiving the Lord because no confirmation of the Word of God was given to them, and there was no clear evidence or manifestation of their salvation.

We believers can confirm our salvation through Romans

10:10, which reads, "For with the heart there is believing unto righteousness, and with the mouth there is confession unto salvation," and through verse 13: "Whoever calls upon the name of the Lord shall be saved." The important point of these verses is that we open our heart to the Lord. "Lord Jesus, I receive You as my Savior." When we confess, we will receive the Lord like air into our spirit. This is the indwelling Holy Spirit, who will be with us forever even if we sin again.

In fact, we need to know that this salvation is the very foundation of denying our self and turning to our spirit. This is the salvation of our spirit, and our soul's salvation is carried out through our entire Christian life.

The Spirit's indwelling and outpouring upon the believers are not merely for the believers but are for the purpose of God's move and His testimony on the earth. Converts experience the indwelling of the Holy Spirit through their salvation.

Many converts also experience the outpouring of the Holy Spirit as in Acts 2. The outpouring of the Holy Spirit is the Holy Spirit descending upon them so that they may receive power from on high. To receive the outpouring of the Holy Spirit is to be filled with the Holy Spirit outwardly. This is the experience of the baptism of the Holy Spirit.

Although the work of the Holy Spirit varies, many believers focus on speaking in tongues. Throughout Acts, glossolalia as speaking in tongues is prominent among the gifts of the Spirit, but it is not the only gift. "Some theologians would argue for the passing of the miraculous gifts,"[98] but in fact, "there is no indication that the Holy Spirit would cease to bestow this gift on the church."[99]

---

[98] Millard J. Erickson, *Christian Theology*, 2nd ed. (Grand Rapids, MI: Baker Academic, 2006), 893.

[99] Ibid., 892, quoted in Donald Gee, *The Pentecostal Movement, Including the Story of the War Years (1940–47)*, rev. ed (London: Elim, 1949), 10.

The Bible also says in Hebrews 2:3–4, "How shall we escape if we have neglected so great a salvation, which, having had its beginning in being spoken by the Lord, has been confirmed to us by those who heard, God bearing witness with them both by signs and wonders and by various works of power and by distributions of the Holy Spirit according to His will?" Through the work of the Holy Spirit, many people will be converted and experience gifts. "Without this work of the Holy Spirit, there can be no conversion."[100]

On the day of Christ's resurrection, He as the pneumatic Christ appeared to His disciples, and they received the Holy Spirit. The records of each disciple who experienced the Holy Spirit may be different. John, who wrote the Gospel of John, and Luke, who wrote the book of Acts, did not have the same experience of Christ. John was one of the twelve disciples, whereas Luke was not.

After the Lord's resurrection, He breathed His life into His disciples, and after His ascension, He poured out His power upon His disciples. But at that time, Luke was not there. Luke's impressions of the Christ he experienced are not the same as John's impressions of the Christ he experienced.

James D. G. Dunn maintained that Luke and John each had a different perspective:

> We cannot simply assume that the Gospels and Acts are all bare historical narratives which complement each other in a direct 1:1 ratio; nor can we assume that Luke and John have the same emphases and aims. They may, of course, but we cannot assume it without proof. At any rate, we cannot start by relating John 20.22 to Acts 2: we must first understand the former in the context of the Fourth Gospel and the

---

[100] Millard J. Erickson, *Christian Theology*, 888.

latter in the context of Luke's thought, and only then
can we correlate the individual texts themselves.[101]

The experience of the outpouring of the Holy Spirit is varied depending on either God's sovereign arrangement or the believer's willingness. Many Christians have the Holy Spirit inwardly and have also entered into the Holy Spirit outwardly, that is, they have the experience of resurrection inwardly and also the experience of the day of Pentecost outwardly.

If believers only understand and claim the visible work of the Holy Spirit, then it will be similar to the Old Testament with the outpouring of the Spirit of God. For example, Samson was set apart as a Nazarite (Judg. 13:5). As he grew up, he was clean and pure according to God's ordination, and he was empowered by the Spirit of God. Although he received the power of God, he was ruined and badly damaged because he indulged his lust. This means that although Samson received the outpouring of the Spirit of God, he experienced no change deep within.

Samson's life demonstrates that the outpouring work of the Spirit does not always change the believers' inner being. Believers need to understand the difference between the work of the Holy Spirit in the Old Testament and the work of the Holy Spirit in the New Testament.

The New Testament reveals to believers that Christ took two major steps, the first being His incarnation, and the second being His resurrection. He took the first step of incarnation to become a man in the flesh. Through death, He took the second step of resurrection to become a life-giving Spirit (1 Cor. 15:45). As the resurrected Christ, He became the Spirit who gives life (2 Cor. 3:6, 17).

---

[101] James D. G. Dunn, *Baptism in the Holy Spirit* (Louisville, KY: Westminster John Knox, 1977), 39–40.

Christ as the Spirit can enter into the believers' spirit and supply them with the divine life and spread His life into their entire soul by His divine dispensing. When we abide in Him to enjoy all His riches, we will grow in His life. When we breathe Him in, eat Him, and drink of Him, His divine dispensing will enter into us to become our air, our living water, and our spiritual food. This is the work of the indwelling Spirit in the New Testament dispensation.

4. Baptizing People in the Spirit and Overflowing Christ with Others

After Christ's ascension, the New Testament dispensation begins with water baptism because baptism fulfills righteousness before God. Before Christ's ascension, in Matthew 28:19–20 He said, "Go therefore and disciple all the nations, baptizing them into the name of the Father and of the Son and of the Holy Spirit, teaching them to observe all that I have commanded you. And behold, I am with you all the days until the consummation of the age."

To be baptized is to be baptized in the name of the Father, the Son, and the Holy Spirit, in the name of the Lord Jesus, in the name of Jesus Christ, into Christ's death, and into His Body.

There are two aspects to such baptism: water baptism and Holy Spirit baptism. Water, the symbol of baptism, and the Holy Spirit, the reality of baptism, are typified by the sea and by the cloud as the Spirit (1 Cor. 10:2) where the children of Israel were baptized. Water is also a means of salvation, typified by the waters through which Noah and his family passed.

The Lord prophesied concerning the baptism in the Holy Spirit to the disciples after His resurrection and before His ascension. "You shall be baptized in the Holy Spirit not many days from now" (Acts 1:5). When this prophecy was fulfilled on the day of Pentecost, the disciples experienced the outpouring of the Holy Spirit

To believe in Christ and be baptized into Christ means to enter into the Father, the Son, and the Holy Spirit and be united with the Triune God. We have been brought into an organic union with Christ through baptism; we have also been identified with His all-inclusive death, and we have been buried together with Him and raised together with Him. This is the union and incorporation of God and His believers.

John 14:16–18 reads, "I will ask the Father, and He will give you another Comforter, that He may be with you forever. Even the Spirit of reality, whom the world cannot receive, because it does not behold Him or know Him; but you know Him, because He abides with you and shall be in you. I will not leave you as orphans; I am coming to you." This reveals that the three of the Divine Trinity are incorporated into one incorporation by Their mutual coinhering.

Jules Gross further declared that baptism is incorporation with Christ:

> Incorporation with Christ has as the necessary consequence of the joining of the Christian to the Father and to the Holy Spirit. The baptized ones are reconciled to God.[102] They are the "children," the "heirs of God, and the co-heirs of Christ. Furthermore, they are specially consecrated to the Holy Spirit. This One dwells in them; together with Christ, He is like the motor of their salutary activity and their new life.[103]

---

[102] Jules Gross, *The Divinization of the Christian according to the Greek Fathers*, 85, quoting Romans 5:10–11.
[103] Ibid., 85.

What God wants to do is to work Himself into His believers and the believers into Himself so that God and the believers are united and incorporated as one. God entering into them and their entering into God are two principles concerning Christ.

Through incarnation, God came into the human race to be a man. His coming is God's entering into the human race. His going is His death and resurrection. These two principles include everything related to Christ and what God does in all ages.

The principle of death and resurrection is to bring believers into God. In incarnation, Christ has brought God among people, and through His death and resurrection, He has brought His believers into God. Through this process, Christ entered into His believers to be with them forever (John 14:16–20).

On the day of Pentecost, the disciples were outwardly "filled with the Holy Spirit" (Acts 2:4), and all the Gentile believers were baptized in the Holy Spirit in the house of Cornelius. Thus, the Holy Spirit did not work only once on the day of Pentecost. He continues to work within believers, and whenever converts are regenerated, He is incarnated into them. This is the principle of God's coming in incarnation.

On the day of Pentecost, the work of the Holy Spirit was clearly revealed. And through the disciples' gospel preaching, the work of the Holy Spirit was made visible to people's eyes. The Holy Spirit continued to come to the new believers to work in and upon them, and the disciples experienced the work of the Holy Spirit every day in the gospel field.

Sinclair B. Ferguson asserted that the Spirit's work is repeatable:

> This is what is in view in Acts 1:8 and evidenced in Acts 2:4. Interestingly this seems to be invariably related to the speech of those whom the Spirit fills.

> They receive "power" to be Christ's witnesses. This elapse of power at Pentecost and the filling of the Spirit, while extraordinary in itself, is not seen in Acts as an isolated phenomenon, or as tied to the specific programme of Acts 1:8. Its repetition does not follow that pattern. This aspect of the Spirit's work seems therefore to be repeatable.[104]

Just as the disciples were not able to understand and experience Christ in a real way before they received the Holy Spirit, we believers today will not be able to understand and experience God's Word in a real way if we do not trust in the power of the Holy Spirit. The power of the Holy Spirit is for testifying for Christ, and the essence of our testimony is our knowledge of Him.

The essence of the power of the Holy Spirit is also the knowledge of the power of His resurrection. Only those who have received the power of the Holy Spirit and the power of resurrection can testify for the Lord. Those who do not know the power of resurrection are not qualified to bear His testimony. For the Lord is the Spirit, and without the Spirit, no one can bear witness for Christ. The Spirit with our spirit is the focal point of the New Testament dispensation.

Once we know Christ and the power of His resurrection, we will spontaneously testify for Christ and spontaneously have the power of the Holy Spirit. The only kind of people who can be witnesses for Christ are those who know Him and know the power of His resurrection.

We believers need to be trained to turn to the spirit. We do not know how to easily turn to the spirit because we have learned to live by our thoughts, knowledge, and experience. Even if we read God's Word and pray, we cannot touch the Lord

---

[104] Sinclair B. Ferguson, *The Holy Spirit*, 89.

unless we turn to our spirit mingled with His. We need training to reject all thoughts and worries and return to the spirit. As we turn to the spirit, we can sense the voice of the Lord speaking from the depths of our inner being. When we turn to the spirit every moment of every day, we have fellowship with the Lord.

W. H. Griffith Thomas wrote, "It is more significant still that it [the New Testament] constantly speaks of receiving Him [Spirit]."[105] By touching the indwelling Holy Spirit and receiving the daily anointing of the Holy Spirit, we can be filled with the Spirit. Being filled with the Holy Spirit does not mean being filled only once. It refers to a daily overflow.

Having the Holy Spirit dwelling within and being filled with the Spirit are two different things. We cannot be too objective and say that we no longer need to pursue the Holy Spirit coming upon us or pursue baptism in the Holy Spirit since we have the Holy Spirit dwelling in us.

To be filled with the Holy Spirit means that the Holy Spirit fills us inwardly to gain full ground in us so that He may be the Lord of our life and of our entire being. Although all the Ephesian believers had the Holy Spirit dwelling in them, not every one of them was filled with the Holy Spirit.

Acts 13:52 says, "The disciples were filled with joy and with the Holy Spirit." The disciples were suffering persecution in Pisidian Antioch, but they were still filled with joy, this because they were filled with the Holy Spirit. If we are filled with the Holy Spirit, then we will be filled with joy because the Holy Spirit is the Spirit of joy. If we are not filled with the Holy Spirit, then we cannot be filled with joy even when we are being persecuted.

The believers in Antioch were filled with the Holy Spirit, so

---

[105] W. H. Griffith Thomas, *The Holy Spirit of God* (London: Longmans, Green & Co., 1913), 167.

they were filled with joy. Being filled with joy depends on how much time we spend with the Lord in our daily life. Ephesians 5:18 says, "Be filled with the Spirit." When we are filled in the spirit with the fullness of Christ and God, we will overflow with Christ.

Regarding the fullness of the Holy Spirit, Mary E. McDonough wrote as follows:

> Emphasize the fact that "being filled with the Holy Spirit," an expression found in the New Testament and often quoted by earnest Christians, does not denote a finality. It is rather an indication of the controlling Power who is filling the personality of the believer. One familiar with New Testament Greek would easily discover that the tense used forbids the thought of the personality being filled once for all with the Holy Spirit, so that no more of His presence might enter. The word picture is that of a pipe connected with a never-failing spring, through which the water is constantly flowing, rather than that of a bottle full of water but tightly corked.[106]

"The Holy Spirit is constantly flowing within us as rivers of living water."[107] The Lamb is on the throne; from the throne flows the river of the water of life, and in the water of life grows the tree of life (Rev. 22:1–2). This is a picture of the redeeming Christ, who has become the life-giving Spirit constantly flowing with the life supply.

The Lord Jesus is also our spiritual Rock in our journey, constantly flowing out as living water to supply us and quench

---

[106] Mary E. McDonough, *God's Plan of Redemption* (Anaheim: Living Stream Ministry, 1999), 81–82.
[107] Witness Lee, *CWWL*, 1963, vol. 4, 131.

our thirst. God's power toward us is the same power that operated in Christ. This power has overcome death and Hades, the place where the dead are held.

In Ephesians 1:18–19 Paul prayed that we would know what is the hope of God's calling, what are the riches of the glory of God's inheritance in the saints, and what is the surpassing greatness of God's power toward us who believe.

Our spirit should be open, our conscience should be purified, our heart should be pure, our mind should be sober, our emotion should be loving, and our will should be flexible. When our inner being has been dealt with, we can know the hope, the glory, and the power, and we will be able to experience the power of the Holy Spirit as the disciples did at Pentecost and minister the overflow of the Spirit into others.

A theology or doctrine without the flow of life leads people to stagnation and causes their faith to easily wither and die. The final filling of the Holy Spirit is not promised anywhere in the Bible. If anyone says he needs no more water because he drank a lot of water that morning, humanly speaking this makes no sense. The stagnant water of the Dead Sea cannot provide living water to believers.

The work of the Holy Spirit is the same yesterday and today. God's good pleasure is that God would become a man to make His people God in life and nature. This is the desire of God's heart, the intention of His heart, and He will accomplish it. This indicates that God's intention is not only with the Israel of the Old Testament. He also has a plan for the Gentiles. For this purpose, God poured out the Holy Spirit upon the disciples on the day of Pentecost. The Spirit of power was poured out on the Jewish believers and the Gentile believers in Cornelius's house on the day of Pentecost (Acts 2:4; 10:44–47).

On the day of Pentecost in Jerusalem, the Spirit descended

upon the Jewish believers, and in the house of Cornelius in Caesarea, the same Spirit descended upon the Gentile believers. We were chosen by God and have believed in Christ by the Spirit. Ephesians 1:4 tells us that we all were chosen by God before the foundation of the world.

We praise the Lord for choosing us in Christ before the foundation of the world. This means that God's heart's desire is for all people to be saved and to come to the full knowledge of the truth (1 Tim. 2:4). If we fully open ourselves to the Lord and receive the gospel, we will enjoy all the riches of Christ that God prepared for us before the foundation of the world.

Christ who dwells in us, His believers, as the life-giving Spirit continues His heavenly ministry by pouring out this life-giving Spirit on us. Through the Spirit we preach the gospel, and by the Spirit we worship God. We praise the Lord, who created the heavens, the earth, and the human spirit.

To worship God in the Old Testament, they had to go to Jerusalem because Jerusalem is the designated place of worship. To worship God today, where should we go? We may think that we should go to a church building. But today our designated place of worship is our spirit. When we worship God in our spirit, we are giving proper worship to Him. Matthew 18:20 says, "Where there are two or three gathered into My name, there am I in their midst." God is seeking for those who worship in spirit and truthfulness (John 4:23–24).

In this chapter, we have dealt with four major issues concerning the Holy Spirit. First, we have seen the history of the indwelling life of the Holy Spirit and the outpouring of His power. When we believe in Christ's forgiveness of sins and receive Him, the Holy Spirit enters into the human spirit. However, in the Old Testament, the Holy Spirit did not yet dwell in the human spirit.

Second, in the Old Testament, we see God's work of leading Israel through specific people by the powerful outpouring of the Spirit of God. However, in the New Testament, we see the indwelling life-giving Spirit and outpouring of the Holy Spirit on ordinary people.

Third, we have seen that John the Baptist's ministry finished the dispensation of the last prophet of the Old Testament through the economical Spirit. However, Jesus Christ filled with the essential Spirit and the economical Spirit, opened the new dispensation of the New Testament.

Fourth, the resurrected pneumatic Christ breathed the Spirit of life into the disciples with a gentle breathing. However, on the day of Pentecost, the ascended Christ poured out the Holy Spirit like a strong wind so that the disciples could spread the gospel and follow Him even unto death.

CHAPTER 3

The Letter Kills, but the Spirit Gives Life

THE LETTER KILLS, BUT THE SPIRIT GIVES LIFE (2 COR. 3:6). THE
Lord is the Spirit; and where the Spirit of the Lord is, there is
freedom (2 Cor. 3:17). When the Scriptures are used apart from
the Spirit, they become the killing letters. In this chapter, we
want to learn how to apply the Spirit who gives life.

The first part concerns the place of the indwelling Spirit,
His address, that is, the human spirit.[108] Believers have a human
spirit, which is the organ for the Holy Spirit and the place where
the Holy Spirit dwells. The Holy Spirit is the person who is the
pneumatized Christ dwelling in the human spirit. A. W. Tozer
declares, "He is a Person. Put that down in capital letters."[109]

The second part of this chapter focuses on the experience of
the Spirit in the renewing of the mind, which is the experience
of personal spiritual renewal.[110] God's intention is to make us a
new creation in Christ (Eph. 4:24). Anyone who is in Christ is a
new creation (2 Cor. 5:17). The old creation is our old person in
Adam, without God's life and God's divine nature (Eph. 4:22).

Christians should be renewed in their mind in order to be

---

[108] Watchman Nee, *CWWN*, vol. 1, 133.
[109] A. W. Tozer, *How to Be Filled with the Holy Spirit* (Chicago: Moody, 2016), 10.
[110] Watchman Nee, *CWWN*, vol. 5, 45.

saved from the old nature. Ephesians 4:23 says, "Be renewed in the spirit of your mind." This is not a matter accomplished once and for all but is something that takes place continually within believers after their regeneration.

The third part concerns the process of sanctification[111] of believers through the transformation of their inner person so that Christ may make His home in their heart (Eph. 3:17). Our heart has four parts: mind, emotion, will, and conscience, like the four chambers of our physical heart. Believers should be pure and not occupied by material things so that Christ can make His home in them. When believers exercise their spirit by calling on the name of the Lord and touch the indwelling Spirit, Christ can make His home in their heart.

In the final part, we discuss that Christians' deification issues in the reigning life. Mature believers experience Christ through their daily life and daily living, and they are purified and sanctified by the Word of God inwardly and outwardly. They are not those who live by their own will, but those who are willing to submit themselves to the will of God. Jeanne Guyon declared, "This is union. Divine union. The self is ended. The human will is totally passive and responds to every movement of God's will."[112]

A. A New Person with a New Spirit and a New Heart

First, the believers' spirit is the respiratory organ of their inner being. Just as people cannot live without daily breathing, they cannot "breathe" spiritually without receiving the fullness of the Holy Spirit. The dwelling place of the Holy Spirit is within

---

[111] Watchman Nee, *CWWN*, vol. 56, 466.

[112] Jeanne Guyon, *Experiencing the Depths of Jesus Christ* (Jacksonville, FL: SeedSowers, 1975), 133.

the believer's spirit. Christ is the reality of the air that the believers breathe. He is also the pneuma, the spiritual air for the believer's spiritual breathing. Spiritual breathing is our calling, "O Lord Jesus," and breathing is never ending throughout our Christian life.

A. B. Simpson referred to this in hymn number 255: "O Lord, breathe Thy Spirit on me, teach me how to breathe Thee in; help me pour into Thy bosom, All my life of self and sin. I am breathing out my sorrow, breathing out my sin; I am breathing, breathing, breathing all Thy fullness in."[113] Christ is the pneumatic Christ as the life-giving Spirit who comes to dwell in His believers' spirit to become their spiritual air, spiritual drink, and spiritual food. Thus, believers live with Christ, are constituted by Christ, and live out Christ. This is what it means to experience the indwelling Holy Spirit as life and life supply.

According to the experience of believers, the application of the Spirit is subjective, personal, and practical. No matter how much God has accomplished for humankind in Christ, unless it is imprinted in believers by way of the Spirit, then what He has accomplished can never reach humankind and become a human being's subjective salvation. The application of the indwelling Holy Spirit is the believers' subjective experience of Christ's death and resurrection and the work of the Holy Spirit in their daily life.

The Lord God incarnated to dwell in the human spirit. The indwelling Spirit is the incarnated Christ, who died and was resurrected to become the life-giving Spirit, who dwells in the believers. The Lord is the Spirit. The life-giving Spirit is the

---

[113] A. B. Simpson, "O Lord, Breathe Thy Spirit on Me," no. 255, *Hymns* (Anaheim: Living Stream Ministry, 1980), 255, https://www.hymnal.net/en/hymn/h/255.

pneumatic Christ; Christ is the pneuma, and the pneuma is the Spirit. The Spirit is the indwelling Holy Spirit who indwells the believers to be their life and life supply.

The Lord Jesus was the first person on earth to have the indwelling of the Holy Spirit. For thirty years, from the day He was born until the time He came to work for God, He lived in God's presence by the Holy Spirit as life within Him.

Isaiah 53:2 says, "For He grew up like a tender plant before Him, and like a root out of dry ground. He has no attractive form nor majesty that we should look upon Him, nor beautiful appearance that we should desire Him." This refers to Jesus's life before the age of thirty. It was entirely because of the Holy Spirit, who filled Him with His life, that He was able to live humbly as a Son of Man in a poor carpenter's house and to walk according to the Word of God.

As a man, Jesus grew up before Jehovah, not as a large tree, but as a small, fragile shoot (a tender plant) in difficult circumstances (dry ground) in Galilee, a despised city in a despised province. He had nothing to boast about or to admire in the flesh, but He was filled with the Spirit. And He was poor in spirit.

To be poor in spirit is not only to be humble but also to be emptied in one's spirit, in the depths of one's being, not holding on to old things but unloaded to receive new things, the things of the kingdom of the heavens. Because believers' experience of the Lord does not take place in the material realm, but in the spiritual realm, the believers' human spirit, the deepest part of their being, needs to be poor, emptied, and unloaded. The Lord Jesus is the Word and is the Spirit. When believers are poor in spirit, they are able to receive the Word of the Lord, which is spirit and life.

The Lord Jesus contained the element of divine life as a

grain of wheat within Him. When He died, this seed of life, as a grain of wheat, fell to the ground. Christ is the resurrection and the life (John 11:25). He has not only the element of human life, but also the power of the resurrection life. As such a seed, with the elements of life and resurrection within Him, He voluntarily fell to the ground and died. The Lord willingly delivered Himself up to the religious people and the politicians, just as a seed is taken and sown into the ground.

In order for the life of Christ, as the Spirit of Christ, to be added into and united with the life of the believers, all the elements of Christ's divinity and humanity must be added into the believer's spirit. Christ, who is both God and man, is the apostle sent by God to the human race on the earth with the qualification that He was both divine and human. He is the Spirit who dwells in the human spirit. Through the mingled Spirit, we experience the Word of God and long for the Word of God in the Bible.

1. Longing for the Word of God

When the Holy Spirit dwells in the human spirit, the human spirit thirsts and hungers for the Word of God. Most of those who thirst for the Word are pure in heart. If they are pure in heart in seeking God, they will see God. Seeing God is a reward to the pure in heart, who shall see God because they are not covered by anything. The Lord Jesus said that those who are poor in spirit and pure in heart are blessed (Matt. 5:3, 8). When believers are poor in spirit and pure in heart, the kingdom is theirs.

When believers feel dissatisfied deep in their being, they are poor in spirit. The Lord said, "Blessed are the poor in spirit, for theirs is the kingdom of the heavens" (Matt. 5:3). Being poor in spirit means that there is a deep dissatisfaction inside. People who are poor in spirit and seek God are blessed because the kingdom of the heavens is theirs.

Enjoyment of the material world causes human beings to indulge in the things of the flesh without allowing themselves to be restricted by God. But when believers are not satisfied with the material possessions of this age and are willing to forsake the seen things in order to seek God, they possess the kingdom of heaven. Being poor in spirit is the first condition of the heart of those who live in the kingdom of the heavens.

The Lord is not concerned about how clever or how dull believers are in their thinking; He cares only that the believers are poor in spirit so that He can enter into them. When they are poor in spirit and thereby open the way for the Lord to enter into them, He enters as the Spirit, not into their mind, but into their spirit. Second Corinthians 3:17 says, "The Lord is the Spirit," and 2 Timothy 4:22 says, "The Lord be with your spirit."

When believers have unloaded their spirit, they make room for Christ to come in. But when they are unwilling to be emptied in their spirit, they put a No Vacancy sign before the Lord and force Him to move on to someone else. When they have a spirit that is emptied and ready, they will know Christ and receive Him as the Lord. Therefore, all believers should be poor in spirit and yearn for the Word in order to understand the Word of the Lord.

In Matthew 22, the Lord Jesus knew that the Jews were tempted to test Him, so He asked them, "What do you think concerning the Christ? Whose son is He?" (v. 42). When the religious people heard the Lord's question, they immediately answered that Christ was the son of David. Then the Lord answered, "How then does David in spirit call Him Lord?" (v. 43).

According to the teachings of the religious, David was the ancestor of Christ. This shows that the religious were in their thoughts and did not exercise their spirit. If David was in his thoughts, he could not have called Christ Lord. "If we remain in our mind, we will be unable to know and enjoy Christ. We need to turn to our spirit and call on the Lord. Only when we are in spirit can we see and enjoy the fact that Christ is the Lord."[114]

The secret to the Lord's question in Matthew 22:43 is *in spirit*. David in spirit called Christ Lord. In order to contact the Lord, experience Him, and participate in Him, believers should take the first step of becoming poor in spirit. The Lord said that the poor in spirit will be blessed in the heavens.

When believers are poor in spirit, they are not in the realm of the world; they are in the realm of the heavens. Believers should learn to call on Jesus Christ in their spirit. They should not care for the natural way of thinking.

When people are in their natural mind, Jesus may seem like an ordinary person to them, but when they turn to their spirit, they will know that Jesus is the Lord. Therefore, believers should first be poor in spirit and then learn to call Jesus Lord in their spirit. Christians try to know Christ in their mind and thought, but this is not the proper organ to know Christ. They need to turn to their spirit and know Him there.

Second Corinthians 5:16 says, "Even though we have known Christ according to the flesh, yet now we know Him so no longer." In the mind of Saul of Tarsus, Jesus was a small man from Nazareth, but when Saul received the revelation of Christ, he turned from his mind to his spirit and called Him Lord Jesus (Acts 9:3–5).

By the sovereignty of the Lord, believers have a willing spirit, but their flesh is still fragile and vexatious. Those who

---

[114] Witness Lee, *CWWL*, 1970, vol. 1, 387.

live by the leading of the indwelling Holy Spirit will experience the working of the Holy Spirit and touch the riches of Christ in their spirit. Those who are led by the Spirit of Christ become pure in heart.

To be clean and pure in heart is to be single in purpose, to have a single goal, to accomplish God's will for His glory (1 Cor. 10:31). Matthew 5:8 says, "Blessed are the pure in heart, for they shall see God." Second Corinthians 3:16 goes on to say, "Whenever their heart turns to the Lord, the veil is taken away."

To be pure in heart is to have a pure and single heart that loves, seeks, and desires nothing but Christ. Such a heart is focused on Christ. Such a mind is focused on only one person and has only one goal. Believers love the Lord and love the saints. However, when they are not in their spirit and live according to the mind, they know that their heart is not pure. Sometimes, they will not be able to testify of the Lord.

Watchman Nee asserted, "Although we do not love the world like some, our hearts are nevertheless affected. We are no different from others. When we do not have a pure heart, we do not have a testimony."[115]

When the heart is single and focused on God, then it is pure. Therefore, the blessing of the pure-hearted person is to see God. To see, in the Bible, is to enter and to gain. In any spiritual matter or experience, to see it is to enter into it and to gain it. Therefore, to see God is to enter into God and to gain God. The pure in heart cover nothing and see God. When the veil is taken away, those who are pure in heart are able to see the light.

Light overcomes darkness. Among human beings, there are mainly two things: corruption and darkness. In order to deal with corruption, salt is needed, and in order to deal with darkness, light is needed. Christians need to be not only salt but

---

[115] Watchman Nee, *CWWN*, vol.8, 125.

also light (Eph. 5:8). But unless they are poor in spirit and pure in heart, they will have neither taste nor light. They will not be able to kill the corruption or dispel the darkness. If believers are poor in spirit and pure in heart, they will be sanctified by the Word and the Spirit and thereby be fit to be used by the Lord.

Peter, Andrew, James, and John were under a great shining light, so they were dragged, caught, and even wrecked. Only a small number of people truly empty themselves and allow Christ to fully occupy them and be built into them.

In this age, God makes no distinction between Israel and the Gentiles. Those who do not have Christ, whether Israelite or Gentile, are not sons of God. The Israelites said to Christ, "We have one Father, God" (John 8:41).

The Lord's answer was very clear: "If God were your Father, you would love me... You are of your father the devil... When he speaks the lie, he speaks it out of his own possessions; for he is a liar and the father of it." (vv. 42-44). Those who belong to the devil are dead in trespasses and sins, but those who belong to God are born of God, they have the divine life and nature, and they love God and long for the Word of God.

When the Lord Jesus gains ground in believers' inner being, He is then able to make His home in their heart. He will also cause the believers' inner person to be renewed day by day (2 Cor. 4:16).

To be poor in spirit does not mean that believers have a poor spirit; rather, it means that they are emptied in their spirit. The way to participate in Christ's ministry is to be poor in spirit and pure in heart. Being poor in spirit brings believers to the kingdom of God, and being pure in heart enables them to see God. If they are poor in spirit and pure in heart, then they are peacemakers and are children of God. Their being children of God means that they were conceived by the Holy Spirit to have the life of God. When His believers have His life and become His children, they spontaneously have the divine nature (2 Pet. 1:4).

2. Love and Fellowship with God

John 4:24 shows that the function of the human spirit is to contact God. For a person to receive God, Ezekiel 36:26 says that God gives the individual a new heart and a new spirit. The new heart is for loving God and seeking after God, whereas the new spirit is for receiving God.

The new heart loves and seeks God. People have a heart to love certain things. People may love food, but if they do not have a stomach, they have no organ to receive the food. Likewise, believers need a spiritual stomach to receive God and a new heart to love God. Our old deadened spirit has been renewed by enlivening it to become a new spirit. And our hard heart has been renewed by softening it to become a new heart.

All humans have a heart and a spirit. Mark 12:30 says, "You shall love the Lord your God from your whole heart and from your whole soul and from your whole mind and from your whole strength." We love the Lord our God with all our being, that is, from our heart. We need to have a spirit to contact God and touch His Spirit. All humans have these two organs, the heart and the spirit.

A proper heart is a new heart, and a proper spirit is a new spirit. Believers should repent in order to have a new heart, and believers are regenerated to have a new spirit. God does not take the old heart and replace it with a new heart; He changes the old heart into a new heart.

Following the same principle, He does not remove the deadened spirit and replace it with a new spirit. Instead, when people believe in the Lord, God as Spirit comes into their spirit to beget them. In this way, the deadened spirit is made alive. Believers now have a new heart and a new spirit, having become a new creation.

A new heart and a new spirit are blessings given to us by God. When we believe in Christ as God, we receive the three blessings of the Triune God: grace, love, and fellowship (2 Cor. 13:14). With love as the source, grace as the process, and fellowship as the transmission, the Triune God comes to us to be our life, life supply, and our enjoyment. When we experience Christ as grace, we love God more, and we have intimate fellowship with the Spirit. When our spirit enjoys the Triune God, our heart will be renewed every day.

When believers hear the word *spirit*, they usually think of the Holy Spirit. They hardly think that they have a human spirit. But it is important to realize that the Holy Spirit is in the believers' regenerated spirit. "The Spirit himself bears witness with our spirit" (Rom. 8:16). Believers have a new heart and a new spirit, and in their spirit, they have the indwelling Holy Spirit, who always strengthens them.

Second Timothy 4:22 says, "The Lord be with your spirit." The believer's spirit is the place where God stays within them, so they are containers of God. Ephesians 2:22 says, "In whom you also are being built together into a dwelling place of God in spirit." The Holy Spirit is the dweller, not the dwelling place. It is the believer's spirit that is the dwelling place. God puts His Spirit into the believer's new spirit.

Watchman Nee propounded, "Ezekiel 36:26–27 refers to the kingdom age, in which God will lead the Israelites back to their own land and give them a new heart and a new spirit. In the church we are regenerated and have a new heart and a new spirit."[116] The Holy Spirit's entering is God's entering into the

---

[116] Watchman Nee, *CWWN*, vol. 44, 892.

believers. When God dwells in the believer's new spirit, He can anoint them, supply them, and work and move within them.

God has given believers a new spirit. The old heart of the believers was hard as stone. Ezekiel 11:19 says, "I will give them one heart, and a new spirit I will put within them; and I will take the heart of stone out of their flesh and give them a heart of flesh." When God regenerates the spirit, He takes away the heart of stone and gives the believers a new heart of flesh, a softened heart. Furthermore, God puts a new spirit into the believers. Regeneration causes the believers to gain a new heart and a new spirit, which is the beginning of being inwardly renewed.

God gives believers a new heart with new preferences. The new spirit gives them new spiritual power and enables fellowship. In the past, they did not like or prefer God's work, did not fellowship with God, and did not understand or do God's work. They had no heart for and no interest in the things of God. Whenever Christians contacted them, they felt strange, confused, and weak. Now that they have a new heart and a new spirit, they not only love and enjoy God's work, but also are able to communicate with God, understand His heart, and cooperate with Him.

B. Experiencing the Spirit in the Renewing of the Mind

Second, for Christian believers to experience the indwelling Holy Spirit as their life, Christians should experience the process of sanctification in the Spirit. Through the process of death and resurrection Christ became the life-giving Spirit. Now the cross of Christ deals with believers' sin. And the Holy Spirit deals with the self through the cross.

The Holy Spirit applies the cross in a personal way to

deal with the natural disposition and achieve the believers' personal spiritual renewal. Renewing comes through the work of the Holy Spirit. The God who renews the human spirit and supplies it with life is the indwelling Holy Spirit, who dwells in the believers' spirit. When believers are touched by the Holy Spirit, their thought is renewed at that moment. God creates the human spirit, gives it life, inspires it, renews it, deals with it, and perfects it.

G. W. H. Lampe expressed this idea that God gives life to a human being's spirit for communion with people:

> The Spirit of God is God disclosing himself as Spirit, that is to say, God creating and giving life to the spirit of man, inspiring him, renewing him, and making him whole. To speak of "the Spirit of God" or "Holy Spirit" is to speak of transcendent God becoming immanent in human personality, for in his experience of inspiration and divine indwelling man is brought into personal communion with God's real presence.[117]

We believers are renewed by experiencing inspiration and the indwelling Holy Spirit. Through God's real presence and through personal fellowship, we are renewed in our mind. The Holy Spirit speaks in our spirit and gives divine inspiration through prayer and the Word of God, leading us to gain more of Him. Our spirit is where the Lord dwells. When our mind is in our spirit, it is mingled with the indwelling Spirit.

When our mind is in our spirit, then this spirit becomes the spirit of the mind. Ephesians 4:23 says, "Be renewed in the spirit of your mind." Being renewed in spirit is not something that

---

[117] G. W. H. Lampe, *God as Spirit* (Oxford, UK: Oxford University Press, 1977), 61.

happens all at once, but something that continues to happen. The more we are renewed in the spirit of our mind, the more the old mind will be put off and the new mind will be put on. To be renewed in the biblical sense is for us to have new elements added to our being to replace and expel our old elements. This is a metabolic process that results in our transformation. Only living things have metabolic processes.

God has a purpose in consuming our sinful body. God raises up circumstances to consume us. He may use our new situation or our weakness to consume us. The more we are consumed, the more we are renewed. Therefore, in order for us to be renewed, we should enjoy God in our daily life.

The old self is old, is sin, and is full of the sinful nature. "All the sins that man commits come from the old man within. This old man is truly worthless, irreparable, unchangeable, incorrigible, and incurable."[118] For this reason, all human beings need Christ, because "the old man is crucified together with the Lord Jesus. We do not die by ourselves; rather, we die together with the Lord."[119]

Every part of our beings needs to be renewed. Not only do our beings need to be washed, but also, we need to be renewed. God's intention is for us to be renewed day by day. In order to be renewed, we need the new addition of God into us. Every day we need to contact God, open ourselves up to Him, and let Him come into us to be a new addition into us day by day.

Our character is the old creation that needs to be renewed to become the new creation. God's intention is altogether to make us new. It requires us to pray, confessing our sins and rejecting ourselves to take the cross of Christ.

---

[118] Watchman Nee, *CWWN*, vol. 2, 2.
[119] Ibid., 3.

1. Being Transformed by the Renewing of the Mind

The phrase *spirit of the mind* indicates that the Holy Spirit has spread and extended Himself from our spirit to the parts of our soul. The work of the Spirit within us is from center to circumference, which means from the spirit to the soul. The Spirit first renews our spirit as the center of our inner being, and then the Spirit renews our mind.

The real renewing of the mind always begins with the renewing of the spirit. When the spirit of our mind is thus renewed by the Holy Spirit, our spirit becomes lively and keen. Romans 8:6 calls such a mind the "mind set on the spirit."

Concerning the renewing of the mind, there are three points. First, Romans 12 says that the mind needs to be renewed and needs to put off all the old thoughts. Second, Ephesians 4 says that the mind needs the spirit to cooperate with it so that the spirit may become the spirit of the mind. This means that when our soul submits to the ruling of the Spirit and becomes united to our spirit, it is a renewed mind. Third, Romans 8 says that the mind should stand on the side of the spirit, be constantly set on the spirit, and heed the move and consciousness of the spirit, thereby becoming a "mind set on the spirit."

When the mind is thus renewed, it has the cooperation of the spirit and stands on the side of the spirit. It then can allow life to pass through and grow out smoothly without hindrance. "The salvation which God has carried out on the cross does not just give us a new life. He also wants to renew all the functions of our soul. The salvation within the depth of our whole being must be "worked out" gradually (Phil. 2:12)."[120]

This change is actually a renewing of the mind. This

---

[120] Watchman Nee, *The Spiritual Man* (3) (Anaheim: Living Stream Ministry, 1992), 546.

renewed understanding and realization is the work of the Holy Spirit, not only in the spirit, but also in the mind. This is accomplished through our daily fellowship with the Lord. As we commune with the Lord, we are filled with the Holy Spirit, and the Holy Spirit saturates our mind with Christ. Then our mind becomes the mind of the spirit. It will be filled with the Spirit as Christ Himself. Therefore, our spirit will be the spirit of the mind.

Romans 12 tells believers what to do and what not to do. We are not those who follow the customs of the world but are those who realize that our mind ought to be renewed and transformed. "Not only does our mind have to be renewed in regard to sinful things, but in regard to our total walk and spiritual life as well. In this renewal we experience resurrection. Originally, the sacrifices are dead. But when Christ lives in us, we have the mind, the thoughts, and the understanding of Christ."[121]

To be renewed in the spirit of the mind is to have the spirit possess and saturate the mind. And since the mind is now in the spirit, the spirit becomes the spirit of the mind. Therefore, our entire being is now under the direction of the Spirit. It is in such a Spirit that we are renewed. Then we experience putting off the old self and putting on the new person: Christ. We are cleansed from vanity, our understanding is enlightened, our heart is opened to the Lord, and our conscience is purified.

All this is because we are in the spirit of the mind. The more we turn to the spirit of the mind and walk in the spirit of the mind, the more our mind will be renewed. Because we have the element of newness in our spirit, we can be renewed in the spirit of the mind as the renewing spirit spreads into our mind. Spiritual work is not outward improvement but inward transformation. We experience metabolic changes resulting

---

[121] Watchman Nee, *CWWN*, vol. 45, 1081.

from spiritual nourishment. We can testify that some inward transformation has taken place in us as a result of our drinking and eating of the Lord.

2. Becoming the Spirit of Our Mind

When I was born again and experienced an inner change in my life, I began to love and long for the Word of God. Then, as I knew and experienced Christ more, I prayed for the salvation of my family.

When Christ, the indwelling Spirit, touched my inner being, spontaneously I began to cooperate with the Lord. Through my preaching of the gospel, I was able to experience the incarnated, crucified, and buried Christ as the wheat (John 12:24). I was also able to experience the resurrected Christ as the barley (6:13). Wheat represents the incarnated, crucified, and buried Christ, and barley represents the resurrected Christ.

When Jesus was on the earth, He was limited in every way: by His flesh, limited by His family, and other people, and by time and space. But the resurrected Christ is unlimited. This unlimited Christ is now within me as the Spirit. This unlimited Christ has enabled me to follow the limited Jesus. I experienced Christ as the grain of wheat and as the barley loaves through the salvation of my family. Through prayer, preaching the gospel, and persecution, the resurrection life of Christ was spread to my family and relatives, and they received the Lord and were saved.

Through this experience, I realized the Word of Ephesians 4:23: "You be renewed in the spirit of your mind." I did not know what "the spirit of the mind" was, but as I continued to pray for the salvation of my family and relatives, I realized that my natural mind was being discharged and was being transformed into a mind that came from the spirit.

To be of the spirit of the mind is to allow the life-giving Spirit to saturate every part of our inner being. Christ not only spreads out into our mind, emotion, and will, but Christ's mind becomes our actual mind, emotion, and will (Phil. 2:5).

Concerning the spirit of the mind, Ed Marks explained:

> Romans 8:6 says, "The mind set on the spirit is life." As we set our mind on the spirit, which is life, our mind becomes life. This mind which is life is the mind of Christ, who is our life (1 Cor. 2:16). This is what it means to be renewed in the spirit of our mind (Eph. 4:23). The divine Spirit mingled with our spirit spreads into our mind, thus becoming the spirit of our mind. Our mind is then renewed with the fresh supply of the resurrection life, which is Christ Himself, who makes all things new (Rev. 21:5a).[122]

When the divine life of Christ spreads from our spirit into the mind, our mind is renewed. With that renewing comes the reality of putting off the old self and putting on the new person: Christ. When we are renewed, our inner being is transformed into the Lord's image (Rom. 12:2).

If we harbor vanity in our mind, it is possible that we will commit any kind of sin. If we have the spirit in our mind, then we will be renewed and transformed into the image of Christ. The mingled spirit spreads into our mind and takes possession of it, with our mind becoming the spirit of the mind.

The believers are renewed by the spirit of the mind and experientially fulfill what was accomplished by baptism, putting off the old self and putting on the new person of Christ.

---

[122] Ed Marks, "Experiencing the Triune God," Affirmation & Critique 1, no. 2 (April 1996), 24.

Putting off the old self and putting on the ever-new Christ is an accomplished fact. However, we experience this and realize this by being renewed in the spirit of the mind.

3. In One Spirit and with One Soul

Philippians 1:27 says, "Only, conduct yourselves in a manner worthy of the gospel of Christ, that whether coming and seeing you or being absent, I may hear of the things concerning you, that you stand firm in one spirit, with one soul striving together along with the faith of the gospel." According to this verse, believers should stand firm "in one spirit" and "with one soul." It is easy for Christians to be in one spirit, but being of one soul is not easy. For example, saints may desire to read the Bible together, but they cannot agree on which book of the Bible to read.

Philippians 2:2 says, "Make my joy full, that you think the same thing, having the same love, joined in soul, thinking the one thing." The salient phrase is *thinking the one thing*. The believers can become one when their thoughts are focused on Christ. Focusing on anything else causes them to think differently, thus creating dissension among believers.

Believers are empty before they are saved. When they receive the Lord Jesus into them and eat of the Lord, they receive all kinds of nourishment. As they eat, they grow and are transformed inwardly. John 6:57 says, "As the living Father sent me, and I live because of the Father, so he who eats me will live because of me." After believers receive the Lord Jesus as their life, they eat Him, live Him, and become the testimony of Jesus. Only the Lord is the Living One who can give life.

When we use our spirit, we understand the Word of God and it becomes our life. The Holy Spirit is life. The Lord Himself as the life-giving Spirit dwells in the regenerated spirit, and we dwell in Him (2 Tim. 4:22; Rom. 8:10). If Christ as life was not in the human spirit, then the human spirit would not be a person but a mere organ. Since Christ as life is in the human spirit, the human spirit is a real person, the inner person.

Second Corinthians 4:16 says, "Therefore we do not lose heart; but though our outer man is decaying, yet our inner man is being renewed day by day." While the old self is decaying, the inner person is being renewed day by day. When our inner being is renewed, we have one soul with one spirit.

In our fighting, our striving, we need to be on the alert concerning our mind, emotion, and will. In the spirit we have the conscience, fellowship, and intuition. These functions of the spirit are not the cause of problems. The cause of problems between us and others is found in the soul. The mind, emotion, and will all give us difficulties. In order to be one soul, we should not remain in our mind, emotion, and will. For example, in our daily life, by preaching the gospel we express our oneness in spirit and in soul.

4. All Things Working Together for Good

The Spirit is a person who dwells in the human spirit. The Holy Spirit becomes the living person of the believers' human spirit, teaching them and helping them to grow in life. The Spirit does not allow such believers to follow the lusts of the flesh and wants them to be formed according to the divine life with the divine nature. The Holy Spirit guides us into all the reality so that we can understand and cooperate with the Word of God.

Gordon D. Fee said this regarding the Spirit as a person:

> The Spirit *searches* all things (1 Cor. 2:10), *knows* the mind of God (1 Cor. 2:11), *teaches* the content of

the gospel to believers (1 Cor. 2:13), *dwells* among or within believers (1 Cor. 3:16; Rom. 8:11; 2 Tim. 1:14), *accomplishes* all things (1 Cor. 12:11), *gives life* to those who believe (2 Cor. 3:6), *cries out* from within our hearts (Gal. 4:6), *leads* us in the ways of God (Gal. 5:18; Rom. 8:14), *bears witness* with our own spirits (Rom. 8:16), *has desires* that are in opposition to the flesh (Gal. 5:17), *helps* us in our weakness (Rom. 8:26), *intercedes* in our behalf (Rom. 8:26–27), *works* all things *together* for our ultimate good (Rom. 8:28), *strengthens* believers (Eph. 3:16), and is *grieved* by our sinfulness (Eph. 4:30). Furthermore, the fruit of the Spirit's indwelling are the personal attributes of God (Gal. 5:22–23).[123]

The Holy Spirit knows the heart of God and, being a person within the believers' spirit, searches everything in human beings. The Holy Spirit searches the depths of people, helping the believers' weaknesses and interceding with God on their behalf. The indwelling work of the Spirit is to bring His divine attributes to human virtues. He wants all believers to be conformed to the image of Christ.

Romans 8:28–29 reads, "We know that all things work together for good to those who love God, to those who are called according to His purpose because those whom He foreknew, He also predestinated to be conformed to the image of His Son, that He might be the Firstborn among many brothers." Believers should use their spirit to actively cooperate with the indwelling Holy Spirit.

The proper and genuine Christian life is a life of dying yet living. Believers should not use their own mind and strength

---

[123] Gordon D. Fee, *Paul, the Spirit, and the People of God* (Grand Rapids, MI: Baker Academic, 1996), 27.

to do something. Believers should exercise their spirit as their conscience and intuition to fellowship and cooperate with the Spirit.

By learning and practicing how to use the spirit, believers can stay in the spirit. They may make mistakes at first, but soon they will learn how to exercise their spirit. Watchman Nee wrote, "A broken man is always ready in his mind; his mind is always ready to cooperate with the spirit. When something happens to him, he does not turn to his mind, but to his spirit."[124]

The Lord Jesus was the first person on earth to have the indwelling of the Holy Spirit. For thirty years, from the day He was born until He came to work for God, He lived in God's presence by the Holy Spirit as the life within Him. It was entirely because of the Holy Spirit, who filled Him with His life, that He was able to live humbly as a Son of Man in a poor carpenter's house and that He was able to walk according to the Word of God.

We cooperate with the indwelling Spirit by denying the old self, which includes both body and soul. This is mentioned emphatically in 2 Corinthians 4:10–12. Paul says that he was bearing about in his body the putting to death of Jesus so that the life of Jesus might be manifested in his body. We have the indwelling Spirit within us, but because we are sometimes stiff-necked and stubborn, God raises up our environment or allows us to have health problems to deal with us. The indwelling Spirit works to cause our will to be flexible.

The Spirit is operating through our environment to consume the old self. Our inner being is thereby renewed with a fresh supply of resurrection life. But without the touch of the Holy

---

[124] Watchman Nee, *Miscellaneous Records of the Kuling Training (1)*, vol. 59 of *The Collected Works of Watchman Nee* (Anaheim: Living Stream Ministry, 1994), 24.

Spirit, our old self is never broken and we fail to experience the renewal of our mind. "After the outer man is genuinely broken, it no longer acts independently. It is not destroyed, but it no longer stands in opposition to the inner man; it is subject to the inner man."[125]

When our inner being is bound, then our fallen-self does everything on its own. The fallen-self acts independently like a wheel turning by itself. When the Lord's arrangement breaks our fallen-self, the fallen-self will no longer make decisions. The Spirit will intercede for us, arrange our circumstances, and cause all things to work together for good to us. When we cooperate with the Lord, our inner being will be free, unhindered, and liberated from the fallen self. We will experience a change in our lives to grow unto maturity.

As those who belong to the new creation, we should deny ourselves and turn to the spirit. However, many Christians have not learned how to turn to their spirit because they are not clear about where the spirit is. The deepest parts of a human being, namely, conscience, fellowship, and intuition, are the parts of the spirit. God's dwelling place is the believers' spirit, which should be filled with the Spirit as the pneumatic Christ (Eph. 5:18).

Although the pneumatic Christ is within us, we need to be filled with Him. We should learn how to be filled and saturated with the Spirit. The saturating is carried out from our spirit through our soul to our body. Our entire being needs to be saturated with the Spirit so that we can be constituted with His elements.

---

[125] Watchman Nee, *The Breaking of the Outer Man and the Release of the Spirit* (Anaheim: Living Stream Ministry, 1997), 36–37.

C. Christ Making His Home in the Believer's Heart

Third, to sanctify is to work God's holiness into believers by God's imparting of His divine nature into their inner being. Sanctification is the addition of the divine element into believers. Walter A. Elwell describes holiness as follows: "To make holy. The Hebrew (*qdš*) and Greek (*hagias*–) roots represented in the Authorized Version[126] by 'sanctify, holy, hallow,' and varied in the RSV[127] by 'consecrate, dedicate,' are applied to any person, place, occasion, or object 'set apart' from common, secular use as devoted to some divine power."[128]

God is working in believers to help them experience the holiness of the Lord. God is working to dispense His holy nature into their whole being. As He is holy, He is working to permeate, saturate, and infuse the believers' entire being with His divine nature.

Christ as the life-giving Spirit saturates all the inward parts of the believers' being with God's divine nature. The Spirit not only dwells in believers, but also works in believers. *To dwell* means to settle down. The Holy Spirit does not simply dwell in the believers' spirit, but lives and works in the believers' spirit. Because He constantly works in their spirit, He spreads the

---

[126] The Authorized (King James) Version of the Bible ("the KJV"), the rights in which are vested in the Crown in the United Kingdom, is reproduced here by permission of the Crown's patentee, Cambridge University Press. The Cambridge KJV text, including paragraphing, is reproduced here by permission of Cambridge University Press.

[127] Revised Standard Version of the Bible, copyright © 1946, 1952, and 1971 the Division of Christian Education of the National Council of the Churches of Christ in the United States of America. Used by permission. All rights reserved.

[128] Walter A. Elwell, *Evangelical Dictionary of Theology* (Grand Rapids, MI: Baker Books, 1984), 969.

divine life into their heart. The indwelling Holy Spirit renews, perfects, and sanctifies them from within.

1. The Process of Spiritual Metabolism

To sanctify is to work God's holy nature into believers by way of the Holy Spirit. The Spirit of God is moving and working within them to discharge the old elements and replace them with the new elements. This is spiritual metabolism, which brings organic transformation to believers. Sanctification is the cause, and its effect is transformation. Transformation is not merely an outward change; it is a metabolic process. In the process of spiritual metabolism, something new replaces the old element.

Ephesians 1:4–5 says, "Even as He chose us in Him before the foundation of the world to be holy and without blemish before Him in love, predestinating us unto sonship through Jesus Christ to Himself, according to the good pleasure of His will." God chose us before the foundation of the world according to His infinite foresight. The purpose of God's choosing us was to make us holy in nature because holiness is God's nature. Without sanctification "no one will see the Lord" (Heb. 12:14).

God predestinated us unto sonship through Jesus Christ to Himself, according to the good pleasure of His will. The purpose of Christ's redemption is to bring us into the sonship of God so that we may enjoy the divine life. The Father and the Son sent the Spirit to make the sonship real in our experience. We have received a spirit of sonship, and we cry, "Abba, Father!" (Rom. 8:15). Sanctification is carried out by the Spirit of holiness. We should be saturated and permeated by the Spirit and live according to the mingled spirit every day.

This sanctification is not only positional sanctification

but also dispositional sanctification. Some Christians have a certain concept of sanctification, thinking that it is Christ helping them to be sanctified, meaning that through their own efforts and with the help of Christ, they themselves can be holy. First Corinthians 1:30 says, "But of Him you are in Christ Jesus, who became wisdom to us from God: both righteousness and sanctification and redemption."

Believers are not sanctified by Christ's help. Christ Himself became their sanctification. Their sanctification does not come from their own virtues but from the person of Christ. Christ is in our spirit. We are turning from our fallen nature to the spirit. It is most important to realize that when we turn to our spirit, we become one spirit with the Lord.

Christ Himself is the Holy One who dwells in our spirit. Whenever believers receive the Lord, we are positionally sanctified, we have been delivered from darkness into light and from the authority of Satan to the authority of Christ (Acts 26:18). When we exercise our spirit and enjoy the Word of God, we are dispositionally sanctified by the Holy Spirit from our spirit, through our soul, and unto our body so that our entire being can be wholly sanctified (1 Thess. 5:23).

God's Word dwells in us, sanctifies our entire being, and makes us His dwelling place to express God. Our sanctification is Christ Himself as a living person. "He does not become our power of sanctification, which enables us to produce sanctification. Rather, we have Christ; therefore, we have sanctification."[129]

To be sanctified (Eph. 5:26; 1 Thess. 5:23) is to be separated from the world unto God and His purpose, not only positionally (Matt. 23:17, 19), but also dispositionally (Rom. 6:19, 22). God's living Word works in us to separate us from anything worldly. This is to be sanctified in God's Word, which is the truth, the

---

[129] Watchman Nee, *CWWN*, vol. 36, 178.

reality. We are sanctified in the reality of God's Word. Christ is the reality of the Word. All the words in the Bible are a means to convey Christ to us.

Whenever we come into contact with the Word to deal with the Word, we have to realize that the Word is the expression of Christ. We need to contact Christ in our spirit as the reality of the Word. Whatever we do, if we do not touch Christ as the indwelling Spirit, then it is not real. "Take patience as an example. I do not have any patience, and I cannot be patient. My patience is just Christ Himself. The same is true with meekness. I do not have any meekness, and I cannot be meek. My meekness is just Christ Himself."[130] Christ Himself is our patience, our meekness, and all our virtues.

Christ is the Spirit now (2 Cor. 3:17). The Word that is the reality contains Christ as its content. To be sanctified by the reality of the Word is to be sanctified by the indwelling Spirit. The Bible has black letters as its outward structure and the Spirit as its inward reality. When we deal with the Word of God, we should not only know its outward structure but also touch the Spirit as its inward reality.

In John 5:39–40 the Lord Jesus said, "You search the Scriptures, because you think that in them you have eternal life; and it is these that testify concerning Me. Yet you are not willing to come to Me that you may have life." Religious Jewish people have searched the Bible, but they have not opened their heart to come to the Lord, so they have not touched the Lord.

To such individuals, the Bible is a book of dead letters because these religious people study and even quote the Bible without the Spirit. If we read only the letters in the Bible without touching the Spirit, then we will find it is a book of black letters and white spaces. A book of letters without the Spirit cannot

---

[130] Ibid., 179.

sanctify us. The letters condemn people and kill them. But the Spirit sanctifies our entire inner being. When we turn to the spirit, we meet the Lord, who is the Spirit, and the living Word of God washes us and sanctifies us.

The indwelling Holy Spirit, who is the truth, sanctifies us every day and opens our heart to understand the Word of truth. The Word sanctifies us, the truth sanctifies us, and the Spirit sanctifies us; therefore, the Word, the truth, and the Spirit are one. John 17:17 says, "Sanctify them in the truth; Your word is truth." This Word, which is truth, sanctifies God's redeemed people and keeps them from the world, that is, the devil. The more truth we have, the more we are released from the bondage of the slavery of Satan, and the more we understand and enjoy the Word of truth.

The truth causes us to be thoroughly sanctified and transformed. Whenever we touch the Holy Spirit, all these matters become subjective experience to us, thus, more sanctification work has been done in us.

The indwelling Holy Spirit not only enables us to understand the meaning of the truth but also guides us into reality. He is the truth of all truth. Truth without Him is doctrine without reality. With Him, truth possesses reality. The Holy Spirit is the Spirit of reality and the Spirit of life. Therefore, the Spirit gives life and makes the truth real to us. Without Him, the Bible is nothing but dead letters without life. He makes all truth full of life and makes it alive in all of us, bringing us into the reality of life and truth.

2. Being Constituted with the Word of God

In John 6:63 the Lord said, "It is the Spirit who gives life; the flesh profits nothing; the words which I have spoken to you are spirit and are life." The Word is the Spirit, and the Spirit is the Word. The two are one. The Word and the Spirit cannot be separated. The Bible has a clear basis for saying that the Word is the Spirit: "It is the Spirit who gives life; the flesh profits nothing; the words which I [Jesus] have spoken to you are spirit and are life."

To give life means to enliven new believers and cause them to grow. Their spirit may be in darkness, but when they receive the divine life supply into their inner being and receive the Spirit, they are enlivened and sanctified. "Life comes from God and belongs to God, so it has to be sanctified through the people who believe God."[131] When believers receive the Spirit by calling on the name of the Lord Jesus, they become holy. The Spirit and the Word of God sanctify and enliven believers.

When believers minister the Word of God to new ones, these words bring life into the new ones. The life-giving Spirit spreads Himself from the believers' spirit into their soul, that is, into their mind, emotion, and will. Finally, He extends to the believers' mortal bodies. Through this spreading, God works Himself with His holy nature into their entire being: their spirit, soul, and body (1 Thess. 5:23). Thus, the believers' whole being becomes completely permeated with His holy nature and is sanctified by the Word of God.

We need both to grow in life and to be transformed in life. Transformation is a profound matter, both deeper and higher than growth. The making of petrified wood is a good illustration of the process of transformation by way of the flowing of the divine life, being constituted with the word of God.

The Petrified Forest National Park is located in northeastern Arizona in the United States, where one can see many petrified trees. Originally the wood is natural, having no mineral element whatsoever to give it the substance of stone. As water flows,

[131] Jürgen Moltmann, *The Spirit of Life* (Minneapolis: Fortress, 2001), 171.

it brings in the mineral element, carrying away the natural wooden element and replacing it with a solid mineral element.

The flow of the current produces an increase of the mineral element and also causes transformation. Eventually, after many years, the wood that has been immersed in the flowing of this current is petrified. This is an illustration of the process of transformation into the divine life.

God's transforming work is to dispense Himself into us and to work Himself into our inner being. Consider again the illustration of petrified wood. There is no wood in the Holy City, the New Jerusalem; there are only precious stones, gold, and pearls. The twelve foundations of the New Jerusalem are layers of precious stones (Rev. 21:19–20), and the entire wall is built with precious stone, namely, jasper (21:18).

In the New Jerusalem, there is nothing of mud or wood, but human nature is either muddy or wooden. We believers need transformation. We muddy people need to be transformed into precious stones, and we wooden people need to be petrified.

The process of petrification is for the water current to flow through the wood, carrying away the wooden substance and replacing it with a solid mineral element. Likewise, when we open ourselves to the Lord and receive the divine dispensing in our inner being, the indwelling Spirit works in us, enlightening us and revealing our unclean nature to cause us to repent and confess our sinful nature. By the divine element flowing into our inner being, the old element is discharged and the new element is added.

When we are regenerated, at that moment we have God's life. But our sinful nature remains the same. We should grow in the divine life and renew our old mind. Transformation of our nature takes time. By our eating and drinking and enjoying the Lord, our sinful nature, our natural character, and our disposition are carried away, and the new element replaces the old element gradually.

The process of petrification is likened to this spiritual reality. God is truly "petrifying" us by being constituted with the word of God, causing the divine life to flow into our inner being. Such a process of transformation makes us precious stones for God's building.[132]

Those who are daily saturated with the Word of God and sanctified by the Spirit are one with the Lord. These people are intolerant of sin and are vessels to express God on earth. These saints have been joined to Christ and have Christ as their authority. They represent God on the earth to deal with the power of darkness and subdue all the evil forces. Jürgen Moltmann states: "The 'Holy' Spirit is the Spirit who sanctifies life, and He sanctifies it with the Creator's wrath against all the forces that want to destroy it."[133]

The Holy Spirit supplies life to believers, renewing their mind and transforming their behavior. "Conversion involves the sanctifying work of the Holy Spirit in forbidding the kind of behavior in which they [the converts] formerly engaged."[134] When believers pray and read the Word of God to gain Christ, the Holy Spirit opens the eyes of their heart and helps them to understand the Word of God. The Spirit guides them to contact, touch, experience, and enjoy the Lord as the reality of the truth. The Spirit ushers them into divine fellowship and communion with God.

---

[132] God's building is the building of God Himself into His believers and the believers into Himself so that they may become one with Him in life and nature, and they express God individually and corporately.

[133] Jürgen Moltmann, *The Spirit of Life*, 178.

[134] Gordon D. Fee, *Paul, the Spirit, and the People of God*, 94.

3. Daily Sanctification for the Divine Sonship

The Bible calls those who are sanctified by the Word of God and the Spirit "saints." The saints are God's holy people, chosen, redeemed, and saved people who live together with the indwelling Spirit. Included with the saints are not only dead mature believers but also living Christians. First Corinthians 1:2 says, "In Corinth, to those who have been sanctified in Christ Jesus, the called saints." Such people are positionally separated unto God by the blood of Jesus Christ. This means when they believed in Christ, their spirit was enlivened by the Holy Spirit. But dispositionally, they are in the sanctifying process with the Holy Spirit working in their soul.

Gordon D. Fee defined the term *saints* as follows:

> Paul's most common form of address to the recipients of his letters is "the saints. "This does not mean they are exceptional Christians, either in the sense of "Saint Patrick" or "Saint Theresa" or that of "my aunt Betty is a real saint." He is simply referring to all the people of God in a given city or region. By this designation Paul deliberately uses a term for God's people from his Jewish heritage. The term *saints* refer to God's "holy people," chosen, redeemed.[135]

Saints means those who are separated unto God, those who are set apart. Holiness is the nature and quality of being holy. Sanctification is the actual effect produced by holiness, the character and activity of holiness, and consequently, the state of being holy to God. Romans 6:19 says to "present your members as slaves to righteousness unto sanctification."

---

[135] Ibid., 64.

Seeing as believers have presented their members as slaves to uncleanness unto lawlessness, now they are required to present them as slaves to righteousness unto sanctification.

Sanctification is not simply an outward positional change, but separation from a common, worldly position to a position for God, making believers partakers in the riches of His life.

Holiness is primarily related to separation, not to sin. The opposite of being holy is being common or worldly. According to Matthew 23:17, 19, what sanctifies the gold is the temple, and what sanctifies the gift is the altar.

A piece of gold in a market is common, but when believers in God wanted to offer their gold at the temple, they put it into the temple with their faith; then it became holy, separated unto God. Similarly, a lamb or goat that is in the field is common, but by faith, when believers in God wanted to put their lamb or goat on the altar, the creature became holy.

First Timothy 4:4–5 indicates that the food saints eat is sanctified through their prayer. All the food items in a grocery store are common, but when the saints buy them, place them on their tables, and pray over them, they become holy.

The Spirit's sanctifying work is also a matter of divine dispensing. When believers first heard the gospel, the Spirit began to sanctify them by imparting Christ as the divine life into their being. Through this imparting, they repented and believed in the Lord Jesus. Since then, the Spirit has been separating and sanctifying them by imparting the Word of God into them.

To repeat, when the Spirit sanctifies believers, He imparts the life of God into them. When they were saved and born again, they received the life of God. Although they have received God's life, they still need to have more of God's life imparted to them every day. This is a gradual process that continues throughout the believers' entire life. No matter how experienced believers are in the spiritual life, this process of imparting life should still continue in them. Then their inner being becomes sanctified and is made holy unto God.

God sanctified us to become His inheritance, which is for us to receive the sonship. Sanctification is for sonship. The sonship in God's New Testament economy is not only individual but also corporate. The only begotten Son of God became the firstborn Son of God, and in the same delivery in resurrection, we all were born to be sons of God (Rom. 8:29).

Sanctification is the divine sonizing. God's purpose is to make us many sons of God in resurrection. His eternal purpose is to have many sons for His corporate expression. God chose us to be holy for sonship. Our spirit has been "sonized," our soul is in the process, and when the Lord comes, our body will be "sonized." Sonship is the focal point of God's economy.

God the Spirit is sanctifying us so that God may impart more of His holy nature and holy life into our being to cause us to grow. We all have to grow in the divine life. For us to be holy, we need a holy element. When the Holy Spirit comes into us, He brings God's holy nature into us with Him.

We grow by being nourished in the life of God. In order for us to grow physically, we need nourishment. In principle, it is the same for the Christian life. God has imparted Himself into us as life. Our birth is a beginning, not a graduation. After our birth, we need to grow in the life of Christ, in the divine life, with proper nourishment in the Spirit. We can be nourished in these three ways: by reading the Word of God, by listening to spiritual speaking, and by praying and fellowshipping with saints. These nourishments cause us to grow.

Ephesians 4:17 says, "Since you have been chosen, redeemed, forgiven, and saved, and you are now realizing the surpassing love of Christ, you should not walk as you did in the past." As those chosen, redeemed, and regenerated by God, we leave the old manner of life behind and live a sanctified life in Christ. Sanctification is God transforming us through His life in us. This is not only the outward sanctification through His blood, but also the inward sanctification by the divine life with the divine nature.

As the Spirit carries out His sanctifying work, He imparts more of God's life into us. This dispensation of life always accompanies the sanctifying work of the Holy Spirit. He cannot impart the life of God into us apart from the work of His sanctification. The imparting of life is always included in the sanctifying work of the Holy Spirit. The extent to which the dispensing of life proceeds depends upon the extent to which He is able to sanctify us. Life imparting and sanctifying work go together. When the Holy Spirit sanctifies us, He gives us life.

God went through many processes to make us holy. We can see God's work through the Old and New Testaments. God is not the same as He was in Genesis 1 or in the Four Gospels. God has been processed by passing through all the necessary steps in Christ. God in Christ created the heavens and the earth and came out of eternity and came into time. He passed through incarnation, human living, crucifixion, resurrection, and ascension; He was glorified and enthroned (Heb. 2:7).

Today God is the all-inclusive life-giving Spirit in our spirit. He is the processed Triune God. The processed Triune God as the all-inclusive Spirit is in our spirit to resurrect us, renew us, transform us, and enliven us with the divine life. Romans 8:10 says, "If Christ is in you, though the body is dead because of sin, the spirit is life because of righteousness." When Christ dwells in our spirit, our spirit becomes life through righteousness. Because of this righteousness, God came into our spirit, our spirit is made alive, and we are able to contact God in fellowship.

Romans 8:11 says, "If the Spirit of the One who raised Jesus from the dead dwells in you, He who raised Christ from the dead will also give life to your mortal bodies through His Spirit who indwells you." We have the divine life in our spirit, but we do not yet have the divine life in our soul. Therefore, we should cooperate with the indwelling Spirit by setting our mind on the spirit and allowing the Spirit of life to saturate our mind, emotion, and will with Himself.

If we continue to cooperate with the indwelling Spirit, this anointing and saturating Spirit will gradually spread Himself from our spirit into our soul. Our inner being will become His dwelling place, and He will make His home in our heart. When we exercise our spirit and enjoy the Word of God, our spirit will be strengthened through the Spirit. Then we will reject our fallen nature, thereby putting off the old self and putting on the new person, Christ, who is living in our spirit.

4. Our Spirit, Soul, and Body Being Preserved

We are the reproduction of Christ as the union of God and His believers. When describing the relationship between God and His believers, three words are used: union, mingling, and incorporation. There is the union of God and His believers. Realizing this important point will solve all problems in the Christian life because every part of the Christian life is actually a part of the mingling of God with His believers. Through this mingling, the Holy Spirit keeps the believers' spirit, soul, and body blameless until the coming of the Lord Jesus Christ.

Jules Gross said: "And what reason did he [God] thus have to implore—with a view to the coming of the Lord—a full and complete perseverance for these three components, namely, the soul, the body, and the spirit, unless it is because he knew that the believers' unique and actual salvation consists in the re-establishment and mingling of these three things?"[136]

First Thessalonians 5:23 says, "And the God of peace Himself sanctify you wholly, and may your spirit and soul and body be preserved complete, without blame, at the coming of our Lord Jesus Christ." The Holy Spirit sanctifies to preserve believers and to keep them away from sin, but humankind's natural thinking and flesh unconsciously make sin. This is the law of sin (Rom. 8:2).

First Corinthians 3:16 reads, "Do you not know that you are the temple of God, and that the Spirit of God dwells in you?" The temple of God is the union of God and His believers. His believers are vessels, and the One who enters and dwells in the temple, God Himself, is the content. Therefore, the meaning of the temple of God is the union of God with the believers, which insight is also the key to unlocking the Bible.

In order to participate in the union of God with us, we should know how to exercise our spirit and deny the life of our soul. The union between God and us can be realized in the spirit. Although most Christians have been taught and trained to exercise their mind, they rarely learn how to use their spirit. A practical way to exercise the spirit is to call on the name of the Lord and to enjoy the Word of God by eating and drinking Christ so as to be one with God.

The way believers exercise their spirit is to deny their natural mind, emotion, and will in their daily life. They are constantly confronted with situations that reveal the need to deny the self and turn to the spirit. Christ dwells in their spirit as the life-giving Spirit. By denying the self and the natural life, believers are giving the Holy Spirit the opportunity to saturate

---

[136] Jules Gross, *The Divinization of the Christian According to the Greek Fathers*, 128.

and renew their inward parts. When they turn to their spirit, the Holy Spirit works in them and renews them.

The Christian life is a union with Christ by exercising the spirit and denying the self. This is the practical way to live in the union of God and believers. Through this union, believers subjectively experience the Lord and enjoy the Word of God more. In this way, they are renewed in their mind and grow in their faith. "However much knowledge you have of the things of God, nothing will ever make up for that personal, intimate, moment-by-moment recollectedness of perpetual fellowship with the living Christ. This is key to a life "in the Spirit." It is Christ becoming your wisdom, your strength, your holiness—Christ and you joined in one spirit!"[137]

When believers are in one spirit with the Lord, they truly live with Him. When the Lord Jesus was on earth, He walked in spirit with the Father. When He spoke, the Father spoke in His words. He was one with the Father, and the Father was one with Him. He wants those who believe in Him to live like Him; therefore, He said, "As the living Father has sent Me, and I live because of the Father, so he who eats Me, he also shall live because of Me" (John 6:57).

The Lord does not simply want believers to live in His presence; He wants them to live by Him. And to live by Him means to live as one spirit with this living One. Philippians 1:21 says, "For to me, to live is Christ and to die is gain." God wants us to live out Christ. This is God's intention, and this is what God desires to do in our age.

To be of one soul is more difficult than to be in one spirit. To be of one soul, we should deal with our way of thinking and our emotion. This dealing must come from the Spirit of Jesus Christ, which is the Spirit spoken of in John 7:39. This Spirit is

---

[137] Jessie Penn-Lewis, *Communion with God*, 43-44.

not only the Spirit of God existing from eternity, but also the Holy Spirit compounded with the Lord's humanity and the living, crucified, and resurrected Christ.

Christ wants to make His home in our heart. In order for Him to make His home in our heart, He should strengthen us through His Spirit into the inner man that Christ may make His home in our heart (Eph. 3:16-17). Christ is in our spirit, but He wants to spread Himself from our spirit into our heart and make His home in our heart. "A man's thoughts issue from his heart (Gen. 6:5; Matt. 15:19). His deliberations—a function of the will—also issue from his heart (Acts 11:23). His joy—a function of the emotion—also issues from the heart (John 16:22). Hebrews 10:22 says that the conscience is in the heart."[138]

Conscience is a part of the spirit in Romans 9:1. "My conscience bearing witness with me in the Holy Spirit." Romans 9:1 and 8:16 state that the conscience is located in the human spirit. On the one hand, the Holy Spirit bears witness with our spirit. On the other hand, our conscience bears witness in the Holy Spirit. Therefore, conscience is a function of the spirit and is also connected to the heart.

The human spirit has a part related to the heart, namely, the conscience. The heart represents the individual's true self. Everything related to our life comes from the heart. The heart is really the entrance and exit of life and the switch of life as well; it has great influence on life. God wants the divine life to spread in our heart so that we may be renewed and transformed and thereby may become the dwelling place of Christ as the Spirit.

Romans 8:6 says, "The mind set on the flesh is death, but the mind set on the Spirit is life and peace." This means that we do not walk according to our mind, emotion, or will, but

---

[138] Watchman Nee, *CWWN*, vol. 60, 312.

according to our spirit. The Spirit will make His home in our heart, occupying our entire being (Eph. 3:16–17).

The Holy Spirit, the indwelling Spirit, renews our mind, encourages us, and fills us with Himself to crucify the lustful body, and the flesh, and supplies us with divine strength and power to overcome Satan's stratagems. As we live Christ and express Christ, the Holy Spirit, who dwells in our spirit, makes His home in our heart by spreading His divine life into our soul. As we enjoy the indwelling Holy Spirit, He will enlarge His dwelling place within our inner parts. Eventually, our entire inner being will be saturated with Christ and transformed into His image.

D. The Reigning Life within Believers

Finally, to reign in life is to reign over sin, death, and Satan in the divine life. There is the reigning life within the believers, but this life has not yet been fully released within them. In order to be holy, believers need to be saturated with the divine life in their spirit.

The way for the believers' entire being to be transformed into Christ is by being daily saturated with the divine life. Their entire being will be saturated and permeated with the divine life and will be constituted with His rich elements. This divine constitution not only transforms them but also conforms them to be the reality of the Body of Christ.

The reality of the Body of Christ is the living of God's life in our mingled spirit and cooperating with the Spirit as the resurrection life. By living in the resurrection life, we will experience reigning in life. The reigning life does not mean that we dominate family members or other people. In the eyes of God, we are all sheep. There is no hierarchy and no ranking.

Although the sheep have different functions, they have the same expression of Christ. In the old creation, we may rule over others physically and mentally, but in the new creation, everyone is all one body in Christ Jesus.

In our human body, the hands, feet, arms, legs, and other different members have but one life and one person. First Corinthians 12:21–24 says,

> "And the eye cannot say to the hand, I have no need of you; nor again the head to the feet, I have no need of you. But much rather the members of the body which seem to be weaker are necessary. And those members of the body which we consider to be less honorable, these we clothe with more abundant honor; and our uncomely members come to have more abundant comeliness, but our comely members have no need."[139]

In the Body of Christ, we build up and serve one another. The problems of divisions and hierarchies come from the fallen nature. These things do not come from reigning in life. To reign is to exercise authority for God, especially to rule all things and deal with His enemy. The proper understanding of reigning in life is that we reign over sin, sins, death, and Satan in the divine life. In order to reign in life, we need to be sanctified and transformed into the resurrection life of Christ. It is by entering into the fellowship of the Body of Christ that we can have the genuine experience of reigning in life.

Entering into the fellowship of the Body of Christ is only possible when we turn to our spirit. Apart from turning to our spirit, there is no way to have the oneness of the Body of Christ

---

[139] Witness Lee, *Holy Bible Recovery Version*, First Corinthians 12:21–24.

and the reigning life. As we build up the Body of Christ and express God in the one spirit, we will have the reigning life.

The reigning life is found in the Old Testament. When we look at the tabernacle, which was built with forty-eight boards overlaid with gold, we see that each of the forty-eight boards in the tabernacle expressed the glory of God. These boards were held together with gold bars that passed through golden rings attached to them. In this way, the forty-eight boards became one. This is the building—the building of humanity into divinity.

The wooden boards represent humanity, and the gold overlaying the boards represents divinity. All the boards were overlaid with gold and joined by gold. Gold is the divine nature of God. Those who reign in life can express Christ corporately by being one and being united by the divine life as gold. Like the tabernacle, the reigning life is not an independent life but an interdependent life. The joining and the knitting are the real Christian life as the Body of Christ. To be joined together and to be knit or interwoven together is to be built together. Through this building, the reigning life is expressed in the corporate Body of Christ.

1. Not I but Christ

The race of faith is not run by drawing on the zeal of natural human beings. This race must be guided by the indwelling Holy Spirit of God. That is why the Lord comes into believers as the life-giving Spirit.

When the life-giving Spirit enters into believers, He brings into them the divine element of God, the experience of Christ's human living, the fact of His death, and the power of His resurrection. Furthermore, whenever the life-giving Spirit moves within believers, He brings them into the Lord Jesus's experience of human life. For this reason, believers can say that when the Lord Jesus died on the cross, they also died. The crucified Christ has been brought into the believers through the life-giving Spirit.

The believer's spirit is the dwelling place of the life-giving Spirit. Galatians 2:20 says, "It is no longer I who live, but it is Christ who lives in me." Christ dwells in the human spirit; now Christ as a living person is in the spirit of those who believe in Him. Believers have both the old "I," which has been crucified with Christ, and a new "I," which has been resurrected with Christ. Believers have died in Christ through His death, but now Christ lives in their spirit through His resurrection. His living in their spirit is entirely by His being the life-giving Spirit (1 Cor. 15:45).

Christ became a life-giving Spirit by being resurrected. As the Spirit, He enters into believers as the pneumatic Christ. Christ as the Spirit constantly supplies His life as His believers' life supply. Whenever believers turn to the spirit, they touch Him, and the divine element is added to their inner being. By Christ's increase in their inner being, He becomes the believers' real person. God Himself, the person of the Holy Spirit, is working with His believers for His expression and enlargement.

However, believers can spread the gospel and expand the church without any growth in life or change in their inner being. If there is no renewing and transforming of their inner being, then any external growth in numbers will bring various problems to the church congregation. Because of a lack of the divine life in the believers, they all will express their natural human desires, which will lead to offenses and many divisions.

God's desire is met by our transformed inner being and by the denying of our soul-life. We need to know what God wants from us. "We must see that God has His need. We are on this earth not merely for man's need but even more for God's need."[140]

God wants us to be His increase in life and nature to express God and live God. Through transformation, we will overcome sin and death and will not compromise with Satan. The Lord passed through a process to come into the world. God was the invisible Spirit in the Old Testament and appeared in the flesh in the New Testament. Jesus, the incarnated God-man, went through a process of death and resurrection. The Lord Jesus had to die on the cross, be resurrected, and become the life-giving Spirit.

In resurrection He was begotten as the firstborn Son of God in His humanity (Acts 13:33; Rom. 1:3-4), and He became the life-giving Spirit. Through Christ's resurrection, His humanity was deified and was "sonized." Now, on the throne, Christ is God and man in the glory, and also Christ Jesus dwells in His believers' spirit. Whenever we want to touch the Lord and want to know His heart's desire, we need to turn to our spirit and fellowship with the Lord through our prayers.

The Holy Spirit is the processed Triune God. The Holy Spirit as the life-giving Spirit enters into believers and dwells in them forever. In the Old Testament, when a sinner approached God without the sprinkling of holy blood, the individual died. In the New Testament, whoever receives Christ as their Savior is redeemed by the blood of Jesus.

When Jesus Christ was incarnated, He brought His divinity, divine nature, into the human nature. The only begotten Son of God came to the earth and passed through human living, crucifixion, and resurrection. In resurrection, the only begotten Son of God (John 3:16) became the firstborn Son of God (Rom. 8:29).

---

[140] Watchman Nee, *The Glorious Church* (Anaheim: Living Stream Ministry, 1968), 11.

Now the Triune God dwells in our spirit. Before we are saved, we have only the human nature, but after we are saved, we receive God's divine nature in our spirit. And through baptism, we are immersed in Christ, taking Him as our life and as our person so that we may be united with Christ as one in His death and resurrection.

Matthew 28:19 says, "Go therefore and disciple all the nations, baptizing them into the name of the Father and of the Son and of the Holy Spirit." To baptize believers in the name of the Triune God, that is, the Father, the Son, and the Holy Spirit, is to immerse them into all that the Godhead is.

Second Corinthians 13:14 says, "The grace of the Lord Jesus Christ and the love of God and the fellowship of the Holy Spirit be with you all." A footnote to this verse reads, "The Son is in the Father, and the Father is in the Son (John 14:9–11), and the Spirit is the transfiguration of the Son (John 14:16–20), that the three, coexisting and coinhering simultaneously, are abiding with the believers for their enjoyment (John 14:23; 17:21–23)."[141] According to the Bible, the Father, the Son, and the Spirit are coexisting and coinhering from eternity past to eternity future. Coexisting means to exist together at the same time. Coinhering means to abide in each other mutually.

Sinclair B. Ferguson attested to the divine dignity and personal authority of the Spirit:

> Perhaps the most impressive testimony to the Spirit as hypostatically distinct yet fully divine is found in his frequent presence alongside the Father and the Son in the apostolic writings. The "benediction" (2 Cor. 13:14) is but one of a series of passages in Paul's letters in which the Spirit is joined fully and equally

---

[141] Witness Lee, *Holy Bible Recovery Version*, 2 Corinthians 13:14, footnote 1.

with the Father and the Son in the outworking of salvation; "the grace of the Lord Jesus Christ, the love of God, and the fellowship of the Holy Spirit" is an impoverished blessing if interpreted in modalistic[142] or Arian[143] terms! It is the unstudied coherence of such statements which makes them such a compelling witness to the divine dignity and personal authority of the Spirit.[144]

The Father, the Son, and the Holy Spirit coexist and coinhere simultaneously. This shows that God is triune. These three are dwelling in one another, and thus are one. John 1:1 says, "In the beginning was the Word, and the Word was with God, and the Word was God." Christ's deity is eternal and absolute. He is with God and He is God.

John 14:11 says, "Believe Me that I am in the Father and the Father is in Me." They are coinhering. The Son and the Father are not separate. They are two, yet They are also one. In existence They are two, but They are coinhering, so They are one. Not only two, but They are three, yet They are one. John 4:24 says "God is Spirit." God is Triune, the Father, the Son, and the Spirit.

The Holy Spirit is the substance, the person, and the Christ. First Corinthians 15:45 says, "The last Adam became a life-giving Spirit." The last Adam is Christ and the life-giving Spirit

---

[142] Modalism teaches that the Father, the Son, and the Holy Spirit are not all eternal and do not all exist at the same time but are merely three temporary manifestations of the one God.

[143] Arianism is an early heretical teaching positing that Jesus as the Son of God was created by God. The argument is that Jesus was the highest created being of God. So according to Arianism, although Christ was fully human, he was not fully God.

[144] Sinclair B. Ferguson, *The Holy Spirit* (Downers Grove, IL: InterVarsity, 1996), 31.

(2 Cor. 3:6). Christ is the Spirit. "The Lord is the Spirit; and where the Spirit of the Lord is, there is freedom" (2 Cor. 3:17). "The Lord be with your spirit" (2 Tim. 4:22).

The Spirit is He who testifies, because the Spirit is the reality (1 John 5:6). The Holy Spirit is called "the Spirit of reality" (John 14:17; 15:26; 16:13). God is a person, Christ is a person, the Holy Spirit is a person, and the believers' human spirit is a mingled person.

Whenever God refers to Himself as "We" or "Us," He is implying that He wants to come into us in the person of the Father, the Son, and the Holy Spirit. For this reason, the Lord Jesus said in Matthew 28:19 that we should baptize people in the name of the Father and the Son and the Holy Spirit. God is united with us in the person of the Father, the Son, and the Spirit. Each time God says "We" or "Us," He is referring to Himself as the Father, the Son, and the Spirit. God is not only the Father and the Son but also the Spirit.

2. Living Christ and Dispensing Christ to Others

The Spirit is the source of life, the expression of Christ, and the reality of the new creation. We have been baptized into the person of Christ; we have been born of the Spirit; and we have been brought into the Triune God—the Father, the Son, and the Spirit. Baptism is a representation of our death and burial. We are united in Christ's death and in His resurrection.

To be baptized is to be put into the Lord's death, burial, and resurrection. Galatians 3:27–28 says, "As many of you as were baptized into Christ have put on Christ. There cannot be Jew nor Greek, there cannot be slave nor free man, there cannot be male and female; for you are all one in Christ Jesus."

Faith brings us into Christ, and baptism brings us out of

old Adam. It is by believing and being baptized that we are transferred out of Adam and into Christ. We were born in Adam. But we were transferred out of Adam into Christ by believing and being baptized. We have become one with Christ through faith.

Just as we are one in the Holy Spirit, we are one in faith. When the Holy Spirit touches our spirit, He brings us into the reality of the new creation. First Corinthians 15:42–44 says, "So also is the resurrection of the dead. It is sown in corruption, it is raised in incorruption; it is sown in dishonor, it is raised in glory; it is sown in weakness, it is raised in power; it is sown a soulish body, it is raised a spiritual body. If there is a soulish body, there is also a spiritual one."

The Bible does not speak of "burying" but of "sowing." People know that there is a difference between sowing and burying. Anything that is sown will eventually spring forth and grow, but anything that is buried is finished; it will not grow. Christ is not bound by death; death cannot hold Him. The Bible tells us that Christ is the resurrection and the life (John 11:25). The Lord Jesus said to Martha in 11:25, "I am the resurrection and the life."

We can see an example of Christ's death and resurrection through the oyster. Through the wound of His death, Christ released His life so that His life could be dispensed into us, and by His dispensing makes us His eternal dwelling place and His expression. The oyster is wounded by sand in the water and produces pearl by constantly secreting its life into the wound.

Now, as we remain in the wound of the cross, the life of Christ flows like the life juice of an oyster, continuing to secrete His life essence into us, nourishing us daily with His Word and His Spirit, and He makes us into pearls. Christ as an oyster came into the world of the sea, lived among people, was wounded by sinners who were grains of sand, and was crucified and died. Christ as the oyster constantly secretes His juice to produce His reproduction as the many pearls. We are His reproduction as many pearls who live in the world as the sea.

In the spiritual sense, the pearls denote how we were regenerated to become a new creation in the wound of Christ. While in the world, the Lord Jesus as the oyster was wounded by us. As earthly people, all of us may be likened to grains of sand. As the grains of sand, we wounded Christ, and in His wound, we experienced His death. In the wound of the Lord Jesus, we died with Him, and in the resurrection of Christ, we resurrected together with Him.

By receiving the Lord's death, we became the new creation through regeneration with His life. Now we live together with Him in the new creation. This is the significance of pearls: we have the life of Christ secreting all the time into us and upon us to make us pearls for God's eternal habitation as the New Jerusalem.

All the grains of sand should be changed by entering into the oyster's wound. Anything of the natural self should pass through death and resurrection by the way of the cross of Christ. All our natural being and all our natural element should become the new creation through the dealings of the cross. Only then can we become the New Jerusalem. The New Jerusalem is not made with other materials. The material of the New Jerusalem is Christ and His believers who are constituted with the divine life and nature of God.

God's divine nature is being dispensed continually into us to turn us into pearls. Formerly, we were sand and clay, but we have been put into Christ and are being molded anew with His divine life and nature. Now we are becoming pearls. In the New Jerusalem, there is nothing of the natural self or of the old creation. The old fleshly I, the natural person of the old creation, should be rejected every day because in God's life and nature, there is no mixture. Revelation 21:21 tells us that the twelve gates of the New Jerusalem are twelve pearls.

Through Christ's death and resurrection, Christ brought us into God. There is death in the universe, but there is also resurrection. Death is of the devil, and resurrection is of God. Death is the devil's torment of all humans, whereas resurrection is God's salvation offered to humankind. Without the resurrection, we cannot be saved and will remain in our sins under death.

Without the resurrection we will be hopeless and under the dominion of death, waiting for the last breath. The best we can do is to eat, drink, and have fun because when we die, we will enter into Hades, waiting for the final judgment of the great white throne, and then be cast into the lake of fire. Without the resurrection, we believers would have no salvation today and no hope for the future. But because Christ was raised from the dead, our salvation today is secure, and our hope for the future is certain. We are the new creation being formed every day in the resurrection life of Christ.

God is a God of life; He cannot tolerate death. He is the God of the living. Through resurrection, God dealt with sin and sins and nullified the death that had been injected into His people. Through resurrection, He has entered into us and has become our resurrection life. He is dispensing His life into us and is removing death and all negative elements from within us every day. This means that every time we eat and drink Jesus, who is the resurrection and the life, the negative elements are discharged simultaneously. We are becoming the reality of the New Jerusalem.

First Corinthians 1:30 says, "But of Him you are in

Christ Jesus, who became wisdom to us from God: both righteousness and sanctification and redemption." As we eat and drink Christ daily as our food, we will be renewed, and His wisdom, righteousness, and sanctification will be ours. Our sanctification is the Living One, Christ Himself. Christ is the living person in us.

Watchman Nee stressed that Christ is our sanctification:

> All virtues are just the different expressions of Christ being reflected in us. Humility, meekness, and patience are not works that we do; they are virtues of Christ. They are the very human virtues of Christ. In fact, they are just Christ Himself. All the different virtues radiate from the one unchanging life of Christ. These different virtues are produced as a result of the many different kinds of environments. Hence, the virtues of a Christian are not different types of conduct, they are the result of Christ being reflected in him. This is the meaning of Christ being our sanctification.[145]

Christian virtues include humility, obedience, and meekness, which are expressions of Christ. But many Christians do not yet realize that they live with a fallen nature, depending on their own efforts and living a soulish life. When Christians turn to the spirit as their conscience and intuition and they fellowship with the Lord, they will touch the Holy Spirit, who dwells in their spirit. When they stay in their spirit, live by Him, and express His virtues, they will become His increase and His expression.

God created man in His own image with the intention that man would become His duplication. The duplication is in God's

---

[145] Watchman Nee, CWWN, vol. 45, 1042.

image, and the expression is after God's likeness. God's purpose is to make man His duplication for His expression so that man may actually and fully be one with God. We need to be one with God in life, in living, and in expression today!

The believers' inner person should be constituted with Christ Himself to express Him and magnify Him. This is what God desires for them, that is, to transform them by the divine life so that their living becomes a testimony of Christ. In this way, the believers are deified, and God can carry out His heart's desire and fulfill His purpose through them.

The believers should be constituted with Christ and have His life and nature so that the church can become the Body of Christ. The reality of Christ is the Spirit. The way to be constituted with Christ is to drink the Spirit. The more they drink the Spirit, the more the divine element will become their constituent and make them the Body of Christ.

We are being reconstituted in life and nature to become God's expression, individually and corporately. The church is an enlarged corporate expression of God. In Revelation 3:8, the Lord speaks to the church in Philadelphia: "I know your works; behold, I have put before you an opened door which no one can shut, because you have a little power and have kept My word and have not denied My name." The Lord said, "You have not denied My name." In the long history of the church through the ages, the name of the Lord Jesus has always been of paramount importance.

The church in Philadelphia exalted only the name of Jesus Christ and did not deny His name. "The nature of Philadelphia is to draw near to Christ, to honor Christ, and to suffer for Christ. The Lord's warning, however, is that every Philadelphian believer has to hold fast to what he has."[146] The

---

[146] Watchman Nee, CWWN, vol. 5, 594.

saints in Philadelphia were overcomers who denied themselves even unto death.

To die means that God wants us to live out the divine life, not our natural soulish life, and to live in resurrection is to live out God as our divine life. God is one with us and we are one with God. This is what deifies us as believers and makes us God in our life and nature but not in the Godhead. The purpose of God's becoming man was to deify us. To be deified is a process that includes redemption, regeneration, sanctification, renewal, transformation, conformation, and glorification.

The result of this sanctification is the New Jerusalem. Without sanctification, God's purpose can never be completed. For the believers to be deified is God's heart's desire, the highest truth, and the highest gospel. God's eternal purpose is that we would be regenerated, renewed, transformed, and built up together as the living Body of Christ to express God and represent God on earth.

3. Expressing Christ Individually and Corporately

The Lord Jesus had the life of God and the nature of God; He lived out God and expressed God in His human living. Now Christ is the Spirit, He is in His Word, and He is living in the spirit of His believers. God's eternal purpose is to have many sons for His corporate expression (Heb. 2:10). We have a Spirit of sonship. God predestinated us unto sonship through Jesus Christ to Himself (Eph. 1:5). Sonship is a matter of life and nature, entirely dependent on birth (John 1:12–13).

God wanted to be one with us to make us His organism by being our life and content to express Himself in humanity. Jesus was God in humanity and He was a man who expressed God in all of God's attributes in His humanity. We can join with other believers in the divine nature. We cannot join with other believers in our humanity. Our natural humanity is the old creation.

God created the universe and humankind. This is His old creation. His intention is not to have an old creation. He intends to have a new creation (2 Cor. 5:17; Gal.6:15). The old creation is in Adam, without God's life and the divine nature. The new creation is in Christ, having God's life and the divine nature. We experience the reality of the new creation when we walk according to the Spirit. Although we still sin in our flesh, our spirit has been regenerated with God's life and nature.

Whenever we turn to the spirit, He touches us and renews us with His life and life supply. This is the new creation in which divinity and humanity are united. The new creation is Christ's heavenly ministry by the life-giving Spirit.

Christ who dwells in His believers as the life-giving Spirit continues His heavenly ministry by pouring out the Spirit on them. Through the Spirit they preach the gospel and by the Spirit they worship God. We praise the Lord who created the heavens, the earth, and the human spirit. To worship God in the Old Testament, they had to go to Jerusalem because Jerusalem was the designated place for worshipping God. To worship God today, we think that we should go to a church building. But today our designated place of worship is our spirit. When we worship God in our spirit, we are giving proper worship to God.

Matthew 18:20 says, "where there are two or three gathered into My name, there am I in their midst." John 4:24 says, "God is Spirit, and those who worship Him must worship in spirit and truthfulness." Truthfulness is simply Christ. Whenever we gather in Christ, our spirit should be released, and we should exercise our spirit to touch the Spirit. Now is the time for true worshippers to worship the Father in spirit and truthfulness, for the Father seeks such worshippers.

When the Lord Jesus came, the dispensation was changed, and the worship of God was changed from a worship in regulations and forms to a worship in spirit and truthfulness. Today in the New Testament dispensation we must worship God in spirit and truthfulness. God is seeking true worshippers who worship God in spirit and truthfulness (John 4:23–24).

By becoming the true worshippers, we defeat the enemy, and we give glory to God. The Lord is the Spirit. Where the Spirit of the Lord is, there is freedom. The life-giving Spirit, the all-inclusive Spirit, is Christ Himself. Our physical life and all the positive things around us are only shadows. The reality is Christ Himself. Praise the Lord Jesus Christ!

When we worship in the spirit and receive the daily supply of the divine life, our inner being is renewed. When we are saturated with His divine life, and His life spreads from our spirit into our soul we have His divine life and nature. This process of spreading and saturation is what we call transformation. This transformation deposits more and more of the divine elements into our deep inward parts to make us the expression of Christ.

Madame Guyon described the transforming of the soul of a human being into the divine nature:

> After all, the changing that is taking place is the changing of something that is in us into something that is Him. Our form has been annihilated in order to take on His form. This is a continuing operation that goes on during the entire life of the believer, changing the believer's soul more and more into the divine nature. This transformation deposits more and more of the divine quality into the deep inward parts of the believer. The soul is being changed.[147]

---

[147] Jeanne Guyon, *Union with God* (Augusta, ME: Christian Books, 1981), 63.

God not only works on us from within, but "we know that all things work together for good to those who love God, to those who are called according to His purpose" (Rom. 8:28). Every time we contact Him, confess our sins, experience His forgiveness and cleansing, we are brought deeper into the fellowship of Christ. When we grow in the life of Christ, the life spontaneously shapes us into the image of the firstborn Son of God (Rom. 8:29).

One of the hymns on God's economy says, "God's eternal economy is to make man the same as He is in life and nature, but not in the Godhead, and to make Himself one with man, and man one with Him, thus to be enlarged and expanded in His expression, that all His divine, that all His divine attributes may be expressed in human virtues."[148]

God's intention is to make us God in life and in nature but not in the Godhead. Second Peter 1:4 says that we have become "partakers of the divine nature." Day by day we should partake of God's nature and enjoy the constituents of God's rich inheritance. Athanasius,[149] who certainly saw the deification of believers as the purpose of incarnation, wrote, "When we partake of the Spirit, we have the Son; and when we have the Son, we have the Spirit."[150] This refers to Christ as the life-giving

---

[148] Living Stream Ministry, "God's Eternal Economy," in *Hymns* (Anaheim: Living Stream Ministry, 1999).

[149] Athanasius I of Alexandria (*ca.* 296–May 2, 373) was a Coptic Church father and the twentieth pope of Alexandria (as Athanasius I). His intermittent episcopacy spanned forty-five years (*ca.* June 8, 328–May 2, 373), with more than seventeen of those years marked by five exiles. He was replaced on the order of four different Roman emperors. Athanasius was also a Christian theologian, the chief defender of Trinitarianism against Arianism, and a noted Egyptian Christian leader.

[150] Athanasius, *To Serapion on the Holy Spirit* (Las Vegas: CreateSpace, 2022), 73.

Spirit united, mingled, and incorporated with the human spirit as one.

Athanasius also declared that God became a man so that we might become God. He assisted in the drafting of the Nicene Creed, and he made the statement, "God became man, that man might become God," which became an aphorism in Christianity for generations. He also said, "The Spirit must be divine because it is he who makes us all 'partakers of God' (1 Cor. 3:16–17—the Spirit's indwelling us makes us God's temple)."[151]

Athanasius referred to deification when, at the Council of Nicaea in AD 325, he said, "He [Christ], indeed, assumed humanity that we might become God."[152] Although the term *deification* is familiar to many theologians and Christian teachers, during the past sixteen centuries only a small number have dared to teach about the deification of the believers in Christ. Dr. Kärkkäinen quoted from Martin Luther's Christmas sermon of 1514: "God becomes man so that man may become God."[153]

God's intention was to become human in order that humans may become God in life and in nature but not in the Godhead. Believers are not objects of worship. Only God alone is to receive our worship. God was incarnated in the flesh. He lived out God's life and not His own life; likewise, we become His duplication in life and in nature and His expression. Just as He lived out God's life, so we should also live out His life. Just as He had one life and one living with God, so we should

---

[151] Millard J. Erickson, *Christian Theology* (Grand Rapids, MI: Baker Academic, 2006), 867, quoted in Athanasius, *Letters to Bishop Serapion concerning the Holy Spirit*, 1.2, 20–27; 3.1–6.

[152] Veli-Matti Kärkkäinen, *One with God* (Collegeville, MN: Liturgical Press, 2004), 26, quoted in Athanasius, *De Incarnatione*, 54.

[153] Ibid., 47, quoted in the Weimarer Ausgabe, 1, 28, 25–32, and in Mannermaa, *Theosis*, 43.

have one life and one living with Christ. God wants us to live Christ by the Spirit.

Galatians 5:25 tells us, "If we live by the Spirit, let us also walk by the Spirit." To walk by the Spirit in Galatians 5:16, peripateo, is to have our practical living and acts in our daily life guided and ruled by the Spirit. To walk by the Spirit in verse 25, stoicheo, is to march in military rank by keeping step, that is, to walk in line. Both kinds of walk, the ordinary walk in our daily life and the walking in line or in rank, are by the Spirit.

The indwelling work of the Spirit brings us into the enjoyment and experience of Christ. The Lord Jesus is the first God-man, and we are the many God-men who follow the Lord. The Lord Jesus is our life and person today. When the Lord Jesus lived on earth, He lived a divine life, and He expressed God. Likewise, we need to deny our natural life through the cross by the Spirit in order to express God in life and nature. Then the divine life and the nature of Christ become our human virtues. Regarding the deification of the believers in Christ, Veli-Matti Kärkkäinen made this declaration:

> "I say, 'You are gods'" (Ps. 82:6). This phrase from the Old Testament, quoted by our Lord Himself (John 10:34), has deeply marked the spiritual imagination of Orthodoxy. In the Orthodox understanding, Christianity signifies not merely an adherence to certain dogmas, not merely an exterior imitation of Christ through moral effort, but direct union with the living God, the total transformation of the human person by divine grace and glory.[154]

---

[154] Veli-Matti Kärkkäinen, *One with God*, 17, quoted in Bishop Kallistos of Diokleia, foreword to Georgios I. Mantzaridis, *The Deification of Man* (Crestwood, NY: St. Vladimir's Seminary Press, 1984), 7.

Christ is God yet man and man yet God. Christ has both the divine life and the divine nature and the human life and human nature, and He is the originator of humankind. His unique purpose in this universe is that we may have His life and nature, and through His life and nature we may be inwardly transformed by the work of the Spirit. God is making us, His redeemed people, to become Him in life and nature. He is making us His enlargement and His expression through transformation with the element of Himself as the divine life. This means that the life-giving Spirit transforms us with His divine life as the element.

Second Corinthians 3:18 says, "we all with unveiled face, beholding and reflecting like a mirror the glory of the Lord, are being transformed into the same image from glory to glory, even as from the Lord Spirit." We will be transformed into the same image from glory to glory. From glory to glory means from the Lord Spirit to the Lord Spirit. This means that the Lord Spirit as the rich supply is continually added into our being.

The resurrected Christ is dispensing new elements into us with all His divine elements for our transformation. When the rich nourishment of the food comes into us, it is discharging the old things and creating a new condition within us. This is what spiritual transformation does.

When Christ as the nourishing element is ministered into our being, this element causes a metabolic change that transforms us. This process of transformation will continue and increase until the day of redemption, when we are fully transformed into Christ's image.

When we become united with the Spirit and one with the Lord, and are replaced by the new element of Christ, our self will come to an end. To repeat, Jeanne Guyon wrote, "This is union. Divine union. The self is ended. The human will is totally passive and responds to every movement of God's will."[155]

God's move is to deify us, to make us God in life and nature, but not in the Godhead. In the four Gospels, Christ was only one God-man, but after His death, resurrection, ascension, and descension on the day of Pentecost, He was magnified and expanded from one to thousands (Acts 2:41). In the four Gospels, God moved with His people, but in Acts, God moved within His believers. Now God and we are moving together, and we and the Spirit are one.

Revelation 22:17 says, "The Spirit and the bride say, Come! And let him who hears say, Come! And let him who is thirsty come; let him who wills take the water of life freely." This Spirit is the all-inclusive, life-giving Spirit as the consummation of the processed Triune God, who has become one with the believers as His bride. But at the end of Revelation the Spirit and the bride, the bride and the Spirit, have become one. The believers are no longer merely the receivers of the divine oracle; they have become one with the divine Speaker.

When we have a sincere desire for the Lord's coming, we have an earnest expectation for sinners' salvation. Now we are waiting for the Lord's coming back. According to the timetable of God's eternal economy, it is implied that the next Kingdom age will begin soon. If we count from Adam until the end of the millennial kingdom, it should be a little over, if not exactly, seven thousand years. Although we may think that this is a long time, in God's eyes seven thousand years are the equivalent of seven days, for to Him a thousand years are as one day (2 Pet. 3:8).

---

[155] Jeanne Guyon, *Experiencing the Depths of Jesus Christ* (Jacksonville, FL: SeedSowers, 1975), 133.

We can say that the seven days of creation mean seven thousand years because the Lord considers one day as a thousand years. From Adam to Abraham was two thousand years, and from Abraham to Christ was two thousand years, and from Christ to today was another two thousand years. We are living at the end of this age of grace, and the coming of the great tribulation will be the transition period before the millennial kingdom.

During the manifestation of the kingdom of the heavens, the overcoming believers will reign with the Lord Jesus for one thousand years. The Lord gives the overcoming believers the reward of a fresh foretaste of the New Jerusalem as the bride of the Lamb in the millennial kingdom. The duration of the millennial kingdom is the Lord's wedding day (Rev. 19:7).

If believers do not overcome, their names will be erased from the book of life during the age of the millennial kingdom. This is not eternal perdition, but temporary punishment until the new heaven and new earth manifest.

We want to stand before the Lord as the overcomers. We have not only the judicial redemption to cleanse us from every sin, but also, we have the organic salvation that renews us through the Holy Spirit. We want to be those who live out Christ and magnify Christ through our daily living. Because of the indwelling Holy Spirit who works in believers, the disciples were changed, Martin Luther was changed, Jeanne Guyon was changed, Watchman Nee was changed, and now we are also being changed.

Praise the Lord! Christ is the center and reality, Christ is the pneumatic Christ, the life-giving Spirit as the all-inclusive Spirit in our spirit. Believers have both the old "I," which has been crucified with Christ, and a new "I," which has been resurrected with Christ.

Now is the time for us to be watchful every day and to set our mind on the spirit, thinking and acting in our spirit. Then the Spirit will strengthen us, enabling us to deny our soul-life, and we will live in the new creation. God's unique goal is to dispense Himself in Christ through the Spirit into us so that He may transform us, conform us, and eventually glorify us, that we may be overcomers to express God in the universe for eternity.

CONCLUSION

The New Testament ministers are ministers not of the letter but of the Spirit. 2 Corinthians 3:6 says, "The letter kills, but the Spirit gives life." The Old Testament law without the Spirit kills people. Without the Spirit, we have no light and will live in darkness. When we are being filled with the Spirit, we will be freed from being under the law and be released from sin and death.

The Spirit who dwells in us is the Lord Himself. Second Corinthians 3:17 says that the Lord is the Spirit. The Spirit here is the life-giving Spirit, the pneumatic Christ (John 20:19, 26; 2 Cor. 3:17–18; Phil. 1:19; Rom. 8:9). When believers receive the Spirit in their spirit by calling on the name of the Lord, many new believers experience the joy of the indwelling Holy Spirit with happiness from their innermost being.

This Spirit is the living person who gives them another life, the divine and indestructible life. A. W. Tozer emphasized, "The Holy Spirit is a Person. Put that down in capital letters." Watchman Nee also stressed that the Holy Spirit is not just a power or a gift, but a living person who is God Himself. And Veli-Matti Kärkkäinen declared that "another Comforter," speaking of the Paraclete, means Jesus is the first Comforter, and the Spirit is the second Comforter. Watchman Nee distinguished two aspects of the work of the Holy Spirit: the inward work of the Holy Spirit is for life and living, and the outward work of the Holy Spirit is for power and ministry.

Concerning the work of the Holy Spirit, there are a few issues raised up by certain scholars. Through these different perspectives, we can learn and carefully pay more attention to the Holy Spirit. First, the work of the Holy Spirit, the person who indwells believers, is mainly for their growth and maturity of life. But some theologians do not pay attention to the indwelling of the Holy Spirit and argue that the Holy Spirit is God's empowering influence. They focus on the manifestation of the Holy Spirit.

Second, in the Old Testament, the Spirit of God was upon people to impart life to His people, but He was not indwelling them because in the Old Testament Christ had not yet passed through the process of death and resurrection. But some have a different view, namely that in the Old Testament the Holy Spirit descended with power within His people, and in the New Testament the Holy Spirit came upon people.

We should remember that the Holy Spirit never indwelled His people in the Old Testament because the human spirit was still in a dead condition due to sin. But in the New Testament, the Holy Spirit is in His believers and also upon them because Christ as the life-giving Spirit can enter into the believers. Not only that, but through the Holy Spirit, believers are able to preach the gospel, baptize, speak in tongues, and heal people.

Third, John the Baptist was greater than all the prophets because John saw the incarnated Christ and introduced Him to people. John the Baptist told people to repent for the kingdom was at hand. Even though John the Baptist introduced Christ to people, he did not have the indwelling Spirit as the resurrected Christ (Matt. 11:11). For Christ's earthly ministry, He was baptized by John the Baptist economically, but intrinsically He is God Himself, and He was filled with the Spirit essentially.

Some scholars insist that John the Baptist's baptism and the

Lord Jesus Christ's baptism were the same, but this is only an outward view. John the Baptist had said that he baptized people in water unto repentance but that there was another One who would baptize people in the Holy Spirit unto life. This means that the baptism of the Lord Jesus was a baptism that leads to being born anew by water and the Spirit (John 3:5).

Fourth, John 20:22 and Acts 2:4 mark the beginning of Christ's heavenly ministry. The Lord Jesus gave His disciples two great promises, the first given before His death, and the second given before His ascension. The first promise was that the Holy Spirit would dwell in believers (John 14:17), and the second promise was that the Holy Spirit would come upon believers (Luke 24:49; Acts 1:8).

The Lord Jesus' first promise, concerning the giving of another Comforter (John 14:15–20), was fulfilled on the day of His resurrection, when the Spirit was breathed into His disciples as the holy breath (John 20:22). His second promise, concerning receiving the power of the Holy Spirit (Joel 2:28–29), was fulfilled on the day of Pentecost, when the outward filling of the Holy Spirit came upon the one hundred twenty disciples (Acts 1:15).

Today, we are not only being saved judicially and objectively by the earthly ministry of Christ in the flesh but also being saved organically and subjectively through the heavenly ministry of the Christ who is the life-giving Spirit. Christ's heavenly ministry is carried out organically and subjectively by the life-giving Spirit.

The application of the Holy Spirit to believers is the process of growth in the divine life. Ephesians 4:23 says, "Be renewed in the spirit of your mind." When our mind is renewed, Christ makes His home in our heart. In this way, the Holy Spirit sanctifies us so that we may have God's holy life and nature, and we worship God in our spirit and truthfulness (John 4:23–24).

When the Lord Jesus came, the dispensation was changed, and the worship of God was changed from a worship in regulations and forms to a worship in spirit and truthfulness. God is Spirit, and also God is truth, the Word of God. Truth is the reality that sets people free. "You shall know the truth, and the truth shall set you free" (John 8:32).

Today in the New Testament dispensation, we worship God in spirit and truthfulness. The enemy blinds us and hinders us from turning to our spirit. Only when we turn to our spirit can we meet God and commune with God because God is the Spirit (John 4:24).

God is seeking true worshippers who worship in spirit by the Spirit in reality. By becoming true worshippers, we shame the enemy, defeat him, and exhibit Christ to the universe. These true worshippers are those reconstituted with the divine life, and they will fulfill God's eternal purpose, close this age, and bring Christ back with His kingdom to the earth (Rev. 12:10-11).

SOURCES

Athanasius. *To Serapion on the Holy Spirit*. Las Vegas: CreateSpace, 2022.

Batten, Jim. 2005. "The Corporate God." *Affirmation & Critique* 10, no. 2 (October 2005): 103–9.

Brown, Robert K., and Philip W. Comfort. *The New Greek/English Interlinear New Testament*. Carol Stream, IL: Tyndale House, 1990.

Clark, Gordon H. *First John: A Commentary*. Jefferson, MD: Trinity Foundation, 1980.

"Did the Holy Spirit Come Upon or Fill the Old Testament Saints?" Never Thirsty. Accessed April 16, 2024. https://www.neverthirsty.org/bible-qa/ qa-archives/ question/did-holy-come-upon-or-fill-old-testament-saints/.

Dunn, James D. G. *Baptism in the Holy Spirit*. London: W & J Mackay, 1970.

Elwell, Walter A. *Evangelical Dictionary of Theology*. Grand Rapids, MI: Baker Books, 1984.

Erickson, Millard J. *Christian Theology*, 2nd ed. Grand Rapids, MI: Baker Academic, 2006.

Evans, Gary W. "Experiencing the Pneumatic Christ." *Affirmation & Critique* 3, no. 1 (January 1998): 54–59.

Fee, Gordon D. *Paul, the Spirit, and the People of God*. Grand Rapids, MI: Baker Academic, 1996.

Ferguson, Sinclair B. *The Holy Spirit*. Downers Grove, IL: InterVarsity, 1996.

Finney, Charles G. *The Autobiography of Charles G. Finney*. Bloomington, MN: Bethany House, 1977.

Gross, Jules. *The Divinization of the Christian according to the Greek Fathers.* Anaheim: Living Stream Ministry, 2002.

Gruden, Wayne. *Systematic Theology.* Grand Rapids, MI: Zondervan, 1994.

Guyon, Jeanne. *Experiencing the Depths of Jesus Christ.* Jacksonville, FL: SeedSowers, 1975.

―――. *Final Steps in Christian Maturity.* Jacksonville: SeedSowers, 1915.

―――. *Spiritual Torrents.* Jacksonville. SeedSowers, 1994.

―――. *Union with God.* Augusta, ME: Christian Books, 1981.

Hui, Archie. "The Pneumatology of Watchman Nee: A New Testament Perspective." *Evangelical Quarterly* 75, no. 4 (2003): 3–29.

International Bible Society. *The New International Version.* Colorado Springs: Biblica, 1978.

Kangas, Ron. "Pneumatic Christ." *Affirmation & Critique* 2, no. 4 (October 1997): 14–29.

Kärkkäinen, Veli-Matti. *Pneumatology: The Holy Spirit in Ecumenical, International, and Contextual Perspective.* Grand Rapids, MI: Baker Academic, 2002.

―――. *One with God.* Collegeville, MN: Liturgical Press, 2004.

Lampe, G. W. H. *God as Spirit.* Oxford, UK: Oxford University Press, 1977.

Lee, Witness. *The Conclusion of the New Testament,* vol. 1. Anaheim: Living Stream Ministry, 1985.

―――. *The Collected Works of Witness Lee.* 139 vols. Anaheim: Living Stream Ministry, 1992.

―――. *Life-Study of Judges.* Anaheim: Living Stream Ministry, 1996.

―――. *Spiritual Reality.* Anaheim: Living Stream Ministry, 2002.

―――. *Holy Bible Recovery Version.* Anaheim: Living Stream Ministry, 2003.

―――. *The Exercise of Our Spirit for the Release of the Spirit,* vol. 4. Anaheim: Living Stream Ministry, 2004.

―――. *The Collected Works of Witness Lee,* vol. 2, 1993. Anaheim: Living Stream Ministry, 2017.

——. *The Collected Works of Witness Lee, 1994–1997*, vol. 3. Anaheim: Living Stream Ministry, 2017.

——. *The Collected Works of Witness Lee, 1950–1951*, vol. 3. Anaheim: Living Stream Ministry, 2018.

Lenski, R. C. II. *The Interpretation of St. Paul's Epistles to the Colossians, to the Thessalonians, to Timothy, to Titus, and to Philemon*. Minneapolis: Augsburg Publishing House, 1964.

Living Stream Ministry. "God's Eternal Economy," in *Hymns*. Anaheim: Living Stream Ministry, 1999.

Living Stream Ministry. "Therefore with Joy Shall Ye Draw Water," no. 1340, in *Hymns*. Anaheim: Living Stream Ministry, 1980.

Marks, Ed. "Experiencing the Triune God." *Affirmation & Critique* 1, no. 2 (April 1996): 17–26.

McDonough, Mary E. *God's Plan of Redemption*. Anaheim: Living Stream Ministry, 1999.

Moltmann, Jürgen. *The Spirit of Life*. Minneapolis: Fortress, 2001.

Moody, W. R. *The Life of Dwight L. Moody*. Westwood: Barbour and Company, 1985.

Murray, Andrew. *The Spirit of Christ*. New Kensington, PA: Whitaker House, 1984.

——. *The Spirit of the Glorified Jesus*. Anaheim: Living Stream Ministry, 1994.

——. *The Indwelling Spirit*. Bloomington, MN: Bethany House, 2006.

——. *The Master's Indwelling*. Monee, IL: New Christian Classics Library, 2018.

Nee, Watchman. *Conferences, Messages, and Fellowship (1)*. Vol. 8 of *The Collected Works of Watchman Nee*. Anaheim: Living Stream Ministry, 1992.

——. *The Christian (1): Meditations on Genesis*. Vol. 3 of *The Collected Works of Watchman Nee*. Anaheim: Living Stream Ministry, 1992.

——. *The Christian (2): Meditations on Genesis*. Vol. 4 of *The Collected Works of Watchman Nee*. Anaheim: Living Stream Ministry, 1992.

———. *The Christian (3): Meditations on Revelation.* Vol. 5 of *The Collected Works of Watchman Nee.* Anaheim: Living Stream Ministry, 1992.

———. *The Christian Life and Warfare: Appendices.* Vol. 1 of *The Collected Works of Watchman Nee.* Vol. 1. Anaheim: Living Stream Ministry, 1992.

———. *The Glorious Church.* Anaheim: Living Stream Ministry, 1992.

———. *Study on Matthew.* Vol. 15 of *The Collected Works of Watchman Nee.* Anaheim: Living Steam Ministry, 1992.

———. *The Fall of Man.* Vol. 1 of *The Spiritual Man.* Anaheim: Living Stream Ministry, 1992.

———. *The Spirit.* Vol. 2 of *The Spirit of Man.* Anaheim: Living Stream Ministry, 1992.

———. *The Way of Deliverance.* Vol. 3 of *The Spiritual Man.* Anaheim: Living Stream Ministry, 1992.

———. *The Present Testimony (1).* Vol. 8 of *The Collected Works of Watchman Nee.* Anaheim: Living Stream Ministry, 1992.

———. *The Present Testimony (3).* Vol. 10 of *The Collected Works of Watchman Nee.* Anaheim: Living Stream Ministry, 1992.

———. *The Word of the Cross.* Vol. 2 of *The Collected Works of Watchman Nee.* Anaheim: Living Stream Ministry, 1992.

———. *Central Messages: Christ Becoming Our Wisdom.* Vol. 36 of *The Collected Works of Watchman Nee.* Anaheim: Living Stream Ministry, 1993.

———. *General Messages (2).* Vol. 38 of *The Collected Works of Watchman Nee.* Anaheim: Living Stream Ministry, 1993.

———. *Conferences, Messages, and Fellowship (1): Overcomer Conference in Chuenchow, November 1935.* Vol. 41 of *The Collected Works of Watchman Nee.* Anaheim: Living Stream Ministry, 1993.

———. *Conferences, Messages, and Fellowship (4).* Vol. 44 of *The Collected Works of Watchman Nee.* Anaheim: Living Stream Ministry, 1993.

———. *Conferences, Messages, and Fellowship (1): Overcomer Conference in Chuenchow, November 1935.* Vol. 25 of *The Collected Works of Watchman Nee.* Anaheim: Living Stream Ministry, 1993.

———. *Conferences, Messages, and Fellowship (1): Overcomer Conference in Chuenchow, November 1935*. Vol. 41 of *The Collected Works of Watchman Nee*. Anaheim: Living Stream Ministry, 1993.

———. *Conferences, Messages, and Fellowship (6): Miscellaneous Messages and Fellowship*. Vol. 46 of *The Collected Works of Watchman Nee*. Anaheim: Living Stream Ministry, 1993.

———. *Hymns*, no. 645. Vol. 23 of *The Collected Works of Watchman Nee*. Anaheim: Living Stream Ministry, 1993.

———. *Miscellaneous Records of the Kuling Training (1)*. Vol. 59 of *The Collected Works of Watchman Nee*. Anaheim: Living Stream Ministry, 1993.

———. *The Present Testimony*. Vol. 56 of *The Collected Works of Watchman Nee*. Anaheim: Living Stream Ministry, 1993.

———. *Conferences, Messages, and Fellowship (5): (Continued) Shanghai Messages of 1940*. Vol. 45 of *The Collected Works of Watchman Nee*. Anaheim: Living Stream Ministry, 1994.

———. *Messages for Building Up New Believers (1)*. Vol. 48 of *The Collected Works of Watchman Nee*. Anaheim: Living Stream Ministry, 1994.

———. *Miscellaneous Records of the Kuling Training (1)*. Vol. 59 of *The Collected Works of Watchman Nee*. Anaheim: Living Stream Ministry, 1994.

———. *Miscellaneous Records of the Kuling Training (2)*. Vol. 60 of *The Collected Works of Watchman Nee*. Anaheim: Living Stream Ministry, 1994.

———. *The Communion of the Holy Spirit*. New York: Christian Fellowship, 1994.

———. *The Breaking of the Outer Man and the Release of the Spirit*. Anaheim: Living Stream Ministry, 1997.

Pember, G. H. *Earth's Earliest Ages and Their Connection with Modern Spiritualism and Theosophy*. Las Vegas: Alacrity, 2015.

Penn-Lewis, Jessie. *Communion with God*. Fort Washington, PA: CLC, 2014.

Reetzke, James. *M. E. Barber: A Seed Sown in China*. Chicago: Chicago Bible & Books, 2005.

Simpson, A. B. "O Lord, Breathe Thy Spirit on Me," no. 255. *Hymns*. Anaheim: Living Stream Ministry, 1980. https://www.hymnal.net/en/hymn/h/255.

Stewart, Don. "How Did the Holy Spirit Work during the Old Testament Period?" Blue Letter Bible. Accessed April 16, 2024. https://www.blueletterbible.org/Comm/stewart_don/faq/the-holy-spirit-how-he-works/05-how-did-the-holy-spirit-work-during-the-old-testament.cfm.

Thomas, W. H. Griffith. *The Holy Spirit of God*. London: Longmans, Green & Co., 1913.

Tozer, A. W. *How to Be Filled with the Holy Spirit*. Chicago: Moody, 2016.

Printed in the United States
by Baker & Taylor Publisher Services